500
dutch recipes

Nicole Holten

500 dutch recipes

From hearty stews and light snacks, to delicious cakes and spiced biscuits, there's something for every palate

Veltman Uitgevers

First Published in 2022 by The Bright Press
an imprint of The Quarto Group.
The Old Brewery, 6 Blundell Street,
London N7 9BH, United Kingdom
T (0)20 7700 6700 F (02)20 7700 8066
www.Quarto.com

10 9 8 7 6 5 4 3 2 1

Nederlandstalige uitgave:
© 2022 Veltman Uitgevers, Utrecht
Vertaling: Claudia Dispa/Vitataal
Redactie en productie: Vitataal tekst & redactie, Feerwerd
Opmaak: De ZrIJ, Utrecht
Omslagontwerp: Ton Wienbelt, Den Haag

ISBN: 978 90 483 2022 6

Publisher: James Evans
Project Editor: Emily Angus
Editor: Julie Brooke
Layout and Design: Rod Teasdale
Food Stylist: Valentina Harris
Photographer: Ian Garlick

Getty Images: Sven Benjamins, 61. Shutterstock: Charlotte Lake , 77; Fanfo 78, 119; Ileish Anna 224; Iryna Melnyk 9; Jack Jelly 142, 172; keko64 277; Maddas 190, 216; Marina Bakes 6; NoirChocolate 10; Plateresca 141; Prophoto42 13.

Printed in China

MIX
Paper from responsible sources
FSC® C016973

Abbreviations used in this book

The following abbreviations are used as footnotes to the recipes:

GF This dish is gluten-free.

V This dish is vegetarian.

Veg This dish is vegan.

contents

introduction

If you were to ask a Dutch person about their country's culinary traditions, they would probably smirk, shrug their shoulders, and say something like: 'There is no such thing' or 'It's nothing special – just meat, potatoes and vegetables.' At first glance, it certainly appears that way. Traditional Dutch restaurants are few and far between, not counting pancake houses or *poffertjes* (mini pancake) stalls. Abroad, they're even harder to find, and if they can be located, they're not exactly vying for attention with French or Asian restaurants.

In all fairness, Dutch food will never win any prizes for its elegance, finesse or refinement. There are no frilly foams, spherified soups or deconstructed desserts. Ours is a plate piled with buttery mashed potatoes, crispy pork belly slices and freshly cooked greens with a dusting of nutmeg. It is a food that comforts, that embraces you with both arms, gives you a warm hug and tucks you in – from creamy *stamppots* (a dish of mashed potatoes mixed with seasonal vegetables, see pages 79–91) to velvety custards, and everything in between.

Herring, often accompanied by onions and pickles, are a traditional appetizer.

Does that mean we don't like to eat exotic foods, spicy dishes or adventurous new cuisines? On the contrary! Eating out is something we thoroughly enjoy. Just about every kitchen in the world is represented in the Netherlands: from far-flung corners of Asia to freezing Nordic countries – if you can't find it here, it's probably not worth having. Dutch supermarkets and food stores are also bulging with exotic produce, interesting spices and hard-to-find ingredients. It is reflective of our love of travelling, of trying out new things.

And yet, ask a Dutch person abroad what they miss from the Netherlands, and without fail they'll mention the food (among other things). They'll wax lyrical about the soup from their grandmother's stove, the bread from the baker on the corner, or how much they long for *oliebollen* (doughballs) at New Year.

But if you listen carefully, it is not just the food they miss, it's also the people – the *gezelligheid*, that traditional Dutch term that is so hard to translate. *Gezellig* is the feeling of finding yourself in a warm, cosy environment, with good food, good friends and good conversation. It's a feeling and an atmosphere that's created by all those wonderful things that make us happy.

So, if you're new to Dutch food, welcome! Give it a try and see how you like it. If you're already familiar with it, welcome back! Remember to visit your favourite dishes, and better yet, share them with others. It is one way of keeping our traditions alive.

Meals

The Dutch traditionally start the day with a bowl of porridge (*pap*, see page 20), or with a couple of slices of bread. The breakfast table usually has a variety of breads to choose from, one or two types of cheese (mature and mild), cold cuts such as ham or roast beef, boiled eggs, and several sweet toppings, including jams, peanut butter and something unique to the Dutch breakfast table: chocolate sprinkles. Whereas other countries use these to decorate cakes, we eat them for breakfast!

Lunch is often another bread-based meal, with a cup of soup or a hot snack, like a *kroket* (croquette, see page 22). A traditional soup would be split pea, called *snert* or *erwtensoep* (see page 48), a sturdy soup made with split peas, carrots, leeks and celery and filled with smoked sausage or smoked bacon. Tradition dictates that the soup is not ready to eat until it's thick enough to hold a wooden spoon standing up straight. Other soups are brown bean soup (see page 45), or *groentesoep met balletjes*, a vegetable soup with small marble-sized meatballs.

Another popular lunch item is the *uitsmijter* ('the bouncer') (see page 15): two fried eggs on buttered bread or toast and layered with cheese and meat. Together with a glass of cold buttermilk, it's hard to find a lunch that is more Dutch.

Our most common meals at dinner time are based around potatoes, meat and

A slice of bread topped with *hagelslag* – sprinkles – is a typical breakfast dish.

vegetables. A typical meal will start with a soup, continue with a main course and finish with a sweet dessert such as yoghurt, pudding or *vla* (custard) (see page 253).

The potatoes can be boiled, mashed or fried. The vegetables are often steamed or boiled and dressed with butter or a type of sauce, and a pinch of nutmeg or white pepper. Most Dutch meals will also be accompanied by apple sauce, *appelmoes* (see page 162); kids especially like this, as it sweetens the bitter taste of Brussels sprouts, kale or chicory. Even though you'd think the potato reigns, it's the vegetable that dictates the meal. When asked what's for dinner, the cook will often only state the vegetable, assuming that the presence of potatoes and meat is understood.

One traditional dish is *stamppot* (see pages 79–91), an all-encompassing name for mashed potatoes with vegetables, which is identified by adding the vegetable's name to the dish. *Zuurkool stamppot*, for example, is mashed potatoes with

***Stamppots* – mashed potatoes and vegetables – are often served with sausages.**

sauerkraut (see page 84). Carrot and onion *stamppot*, or *hutspot* (see page 83), is one of the few exceptions but only in name: it is said that *hutspot* is eaten at least once a week in traditional Dutch households.

As for meats, the Dutch like to eat *braadworst*, a fresh, coiled pork sausage; *gehaktballen* (meatballs) (see page 100); tender stewed beef called *draadjesvlees* (the meat is so tender it falls apart in threads, *draadjes*) (see page 99); and pork belly slices, *speklappen* (see page 105).

Dessert is often yoghurt with fresh fruit, or the more traditional *vla*: a type of custard that comes in over 20 flavours (see page 253). Some of the most popular are vanilla, lemon, chocolate and *Hopjes*, with the flavour of that famous coffee candy from The Hague. An old-fashioned dessert is *griesmeelpudding* (see page 251), made with semolina and milk, and served with a berry sauce.

Lastly, we love our coffee. It is still traditional to grab a cup of coffee around 10.30 in the morning with a co-worker or a friend, and do the same thing around 4pm. And coffee or tea is often accompanied by something sweet; a glance at our bakeries and grocery aisles reveals an impressive selection of baked goods: cakes, sweet breads, cookies, tarts and pies. Birthday parties start with a round of coffee and cake, and it's not unusual for families to share a cup of coffee and cookies or pie around 8pm in front of the TV: *gezellig!*

Influences

As small as our country is, our regional cuisines consist of a wide variety of dishes, many of which are rich in both ingredients and history. The agricultural availability and production of foods heavily influenced these provincial recipes. Limburg, for example, is famous for traditional fruit pies (see page 241), white asparagus (see page 143), *zuurvlees* (beef stew) (see page 95) and thick apple molasses. In the north, Friesland has a rich baking tradition, with *sûkerbôle* (sugar bread) (see page 189), *dumkes* (spiced cookies) (see page 214) and *oranjekoek* (orange cake); Groningen on the eastern border is famous for its mustard; and Zeeland on the west coast has excellent seafood.

Dutch cuisine is also influenced by centuries of travel, of exploring other worlds, but also by the presence of the world on our doorstep. It is not uncommon to find a Middle Eastern greengrocer, a Polish supermarket, an Irish pub and an Indonesian *toko*, all in one city block. And just about every other small town has at least one Chinese-Indonesian restaurant, a shawarma place and a pizza parlour.

The culinary influences from our overseas involvement in Indonesia, Suriname and the Antillean islands can also be found all around us: Indonesian dishes like *nasi goreng* (see page 110) and *satay* (see page 113) have almost become a staple at home, and the Surinamese *roti kip* is quickly becoming a national favourite, too. One of our most popular *stamppots*, the *hutspot*, is said to be a remnant of the Spanish occupation during the sixteenth century. Other influences on our regional cuisines date from the Middle Ages, when the bustling commerce along the Hanseatic cities encouraged the production and purchasing of grains, wine, salt and spices.

Equipment

As Dutch cuisine is so practical and straightforward, you probably already own most of the equipment that you need. However, several items will make preparing our food a lot easier. A potato masher, preferably stainless steel with a zigzag wire pattern, will make easy work of *stamppots*. A large frying pan is useful for pancakes, and for our warm dairy desserts it would be worthwhile having a pan with a heavy bottom, to keep the milk from burning. Stews will do great well in cast-iron casseroles, and for some of the meat dishes a heat diffuser is a great asset.

In addition, a large stockpot, knives, cutting boards, a colander, a stick blender, a potato peeler and a cheese slicer will come in handy, as well as baking sheets, springform cake tins and a set of measuring spoons.

Cling film, aluminium foil, a mixed set of bowls and oven dishes, whisks and spatulas will also be useful.

Lastly, a *poffertjespan*, a dimpled cast-iron frying pan, used to make these small pancakes (see page 246) is great, but not imperative. A frying pan will work instead.

Ingredients

Most of the ingredients used in this book are readily available from your supermarket. Here are some tips to help you to achieve authentic dishes:

- Use floury potatoes such as Desiree, King Edward or Maris Piper, especially if you are making *stamppot*.
- The smoked rope sausage or smoked pork sausage can be substituted with *kielbasa*, large hotdogs, or a vegetarian or vegan smoked product.
- Where milk is used, for best flavour and texture, use whole milk if you can. However, most dairy recipes can also use oat, nut or soy milk.
- The recipes have been created using unsalted butter, but if you do choose salted butter, you may want to omit additional salt, even if the recipe calls for it.
- At the end, taste and adjust the seasoning to your own taste.

Dutch cuisine makes good use of the country's traditional sausages.

light meals, soups & salads

A hot cup of split pea soup on a winter's day, a delicious *kroket* on a soft white roll for lunch, or a traditional Dutch potato salad with a creamy dressing and a few pieces of toast: as simple as some of these Dutch dishes may seem, we value quality over quantity, and still prefer homemade over store-bought.

fried eggs on bread

see variations pago 55

This dish – two fried eggs on slices of buttered bread – earned its name *uitsmijter* from being the signature dish eaten when it was time to go home after a night of partying: '*uitsmijter*' is the word for 'bouncer'. Nowadays, it has evolved into a delicious lunch, complete with a small tomato salad on the side.

2 slices buttered bread
2 slices cooked ham
2 slices mature cheese (such as Cheddar or Gouda)
2 tbsp butter
2 eggs
1 large ripe tomato
salt and freshly ground black pepper

Place the slices of bread on a plate, buttered side up. Add a slice of ham, then a slice of cheese to each one.

Melt the butter in a frying pan and fry both eggs, sunny side up, for 3 minutes (white set, runny yolk) to 5 minutes (yolk set). Carefully place the fried eggs on top of the cheese.

Slice the tomato into six equal pieces, season with salt and pepper and serve alongside the bread.

Serves 1

GF Use gluten-free bread.

devilled eggs

see variations page 56

Devilled eggs (*gevulde eieren*) are such a classic treat, and with modern flavours they continue to be popular. They are delicious served with a slice of bread and butter.

4 eggs
60g butter, melted
1/4 tsp yellow or stoneground mustard
3 sprigs of fresh chives, chopped
salt and freshly ground black pepper, to taste
pinch of cayenne pepper

Boil the eggs for 8 minutes, then leave to cool. Peel the eggs, then slice them in half lengthways and carefully scoop out the yolks. Mash the yolks in a bowl with the melted butter and season with the mustard, salt and pepper. Fold in half of the chopped chives.

Use a small spoon to fill the cavity of the eggs with the yolk mixture. Top with a light dusting of cayenne and a sprinkling of the remaining chives.

Serves 4

GF Use gluten-free mustard. **V**

savoury tart

see variations page 57

Savoury tarts (*hartige taart*) baked in a puff pastry crust are a welcome lunch choice, hot or cold, served with a tomato salad or a green salad on the side.

1 x 320g (11oz) packet of ready rolled puff pastry
4 eggs
100ml (3½fl oz) double cream
250g (9oz) tenderstem broccoli
125g (4½oz) cooked ham, cubed
75g (2¾oz) mature Cheddar, grated
butter or oil spray, for greasing

Preheat the oven to 200°C (400°F).

Grease a 23cm (9in) tart pan, line with the puff pastry and trim the edges.

Beat the eggs in a bowl with the cream. Slice the broccoli in half lengthways, rinse and dry. Divide the broccoli and ham equally over the puff pastry base and carefully pour the egg mixture over it. Sprinkle the cheese on top.

Bake on the middle shelf for 25–30 minutes, until cooked through and the eggs are set.

Serves 4–6

GF Use gluten-free pastry.

flour porridge

see variations page 58

We are raised on flour porridge (*meelpap*) as children, but many adults still eat it as a hot breakfast for that extra boost of energy in the morning, or chilled as a welcome variation on dessert. This dish can also be made with different milks such as almond, soy or oat. Beer porridge is usually consumed in the evening, for dinner or dessert.

1 litre (1¾ pints) milk
75g (2¾oz) plain flour
1 small lemon
pinch of salt
1 tbsp brown sugar

Mix 100ml (3½fl oz) of the milk with the flour to form a paste, stirring well to remove any lumps.

Using a sharp knife or a potato peeler, cut a strip of zest from the lemon, about 6–7cm (2¼–2¾in) long. Add it to the remainder of the milk in a pan and bring to the boil. Stir in the flour paste, reduce the heat to a simmer and continue to stir for 2–3 minutes, until the porridge has thickened.

Before serving, remove the lemon zest and add a pinch of salt then stir through the brown sugar.

Serves 4

GF Use gluten-free flour. **V Veg** Use non-dairy milk.

beef croquettes

see variations page 59

Kroketten (croquettes) started out as a fancy way to use up leftovers: meat was made into a creamy ragout, which was rolled into short logs, covered in breadcrumbs and deep-fried. Nowadays there are many varieties of this snack. The smaller round version of the *kroket* is the *bitterbal*, a popular choice to accompany a beer on a night out.

35g (1¼oz) butter
35g (1¼oz) plain flour, plus extra for coating
250ml (8¾fl oz) beef or veal stock
200g (7oz) cooked beef or veal, shredded or finely chopped
pinch of dried thyme
handful of fresh parsley, chopped
2 eggs
150g (5¼oz) dried or panko breadcrumbs
sunflower or rapeseed oil, for frying
freshly ground black pepper
yellow or stoneground mustard, to serve

Melt the butter in a frying pan and stir in the flour until it becomes a thick paste. Add the stock one ladleful at a time, stirring constantly and making sure all the liquid is absorbed before adding the next. Fold in the meat, thyme, parsley and a pinch of black pepper and cook for an additional 2 minutes while stirring. Line a shallow dish with cling film and spread the mixture out thinly. Cover with cling film and let it cool overnight.

The next day, divide the paste into eight equal pieces. Sprinkle some flour on the work surface and roll each piece into a log, about 10cm (4in) long and 3cm (1¼in) thick. (For *bitterballen*, divide into 24 equal pieces and roll into large marbles.) Beat the eggs in a bowl. Line up another two bowls: one with flour and one with the breadcrumbs. Roll a log lightly through the flour. Shake or brush off the excess, then roll through the egg,

making sure it's covered on all sides (a fork will help). Lift it out, tap lightly and roll it through the breadcrumbs. Do this with all eight croquettes. Refrigerate them for 30 minutes, and in the meantime heat the oil in a deep-fat fryer to 180°C (350°F). Roll the logs through the egg and breadcrumbs one more time. Fry two croquettes at a time, for 3–5 minutes, until golden brown. Drain on kitchen towel and serve with a squeeze of mustard. Be careful, as they will be hot!

Serves 4

GF Use gluten-free mustard, flour and breadcrumbs.

omelette

see variations page 60

Lunch often consists of something hot: a cup of soup, a *kroket* (croquette, see page 22) or a savoury *omelet* (omelette). Pair them with two slices of buttered wholemeal bread and you're ready to tackle the rest of the day!

2 eggs
1 tbsp butter, plus extra for the bread
salt and freshly ground black pepper
2 slices wholemeal bread

Beat the eggs in a bowl and add a sprinkle of salt.

Heat the butter in a small non-stick frying pan over a low-medium heat until it foams. Pour in the eggs and swirl the pan slightly until the eggs cover the whole surface.

Using a heat-resistant spatula, bring the sides of the omelette towards the middle, letting the uncooked egg fill the void. Continue to do this until the top is almost cooked through, 7–8 minutes, then use the spatula to fold the omelette in half.

Butter two slices of wholemeal bread, place the omelette on the bread and sprinkle with freshly ground black pepper.

Serves 1

GF Use gluten-free bread. **V**

chicken vol-au-vents

see variations page 61

A *pasteitje met ragout* makes the perfect starter for a holiday meal, lunch or early dinner. The pastry shells can be bought ready-made at the supermarket.

1kg (2lb 3oz) chicken thighs, legs and breast
1 small onion, halved
3 bay leaves
100g (3½oz) butter
125g (4½oz) white button mushrooms, sliced
pinch of dried thyme
80ml (2¾fl oz) dry white wine
2 tbsp double cream
75g (2¾oz) plain flour
1 chicken stock cube
small handful chopped fresh parsley
4 readymade vol-au-vent cases, cooked according to the packet instructions
salt and freshly ground black pepper

Add 1 litre (1¾ pints) water to a pan with the chicken, onion and bay leaves and simmer for 45 minutes, or until the chicken is cooked. Remove the chicken and strain the liquid – you should have about 700ml (25fl oz) stock (if not, make up the difference with water or stock). Discard the onion and bay leaves. Remove the meat from the chicken and cut it into bite-sized pieces. Melt 25g (¾oz) of the butter in a frying pan and sauté the mushrooms and thyme with a pinch of salt and pepper until softened, about 3 minutes. Set aside in a bowl. Pour the wine into the warm pan and scrape the base with a wooden spoon to release the sediment. Bring to the boil and cook until reduced by half, about 2 minutes, then add to the mushrooms. In the same pan, melt the remaining butter and stir in the flour to create a thick paste. Add 1 ladleful of stock at a time, stirring constantly, until all the liquid is incorporated. Stir in the stock cube. Fold the chicken, mushrooms and cream into the sauce and adjust the seasoning. Divide the mixture between the vol-au-vent cases and sprinkle with parsley.

Serves 4

sausage bread rolls

see variations page 62

Just like the sausage rolls with puff pastry (see page 29), *worstenbroodje* make a delicious lunch or late-night snack, and are so easy to make. They can be served with tomato ketchup.

1 tsp dried active yeast
175ml (6fl oz) warm milk
250g (9oz) plain flour
1/4 tsp salt
30g (1oz) butter, melted
3 eggs
250g (9oz) minced beef
250g (9oz) minced pork
1/4 tsp freshly ground white pepper
2 tsp flaky sea salt
1/4 tsp ground nutmeg
75g (2 3/4oz) dried or panko breadcrumbs
handful of chopped fresh parsley
4 tbsp cold milk

Stir the yeast into the warm milk and let sit for 10 minutes, or until bubbly. Add the flour and salt and start mixing the dough. Drizzle the butter over the top, continuing to mix, and finally add 1 egg, beaten. Mix briefly until it all comes together, then knead by hand for 10 minutes, or until supple and soft. Cover and let rise until about doubled in size, 30–40 minutes. Combine the meats with the spices, breadcrumbs, 1 egg, the parsley and the cold milk. Divide into 55g (2oz) portions and roll into small sausages about 13cm (5in) long.

Line a baking sheet with parchment paper. Punch down the dough and divide into 55g (2oz) pieces. Roll each piece into a ball and, using a rolling pin, roll into ovals, about 15cm (6in) long. Place a sausage on top, fold over the short edges, pull over a long edge and carefully roll the sausage over in the dough. Pinch the seam. Place on the prepared baking sheet spaced 3–5cm (1 1/2–2in) apart. Cover the sausage rolls and let them rise until puffy, and the dough does not spring back when you poke it with a finger, about 20 minutes. Mix the third

egg with 2 tablespoons of water. Preheat the oven to 190°C (375°F). Brush the sausage rolls with the egg mixture and bake for 20–30 minutes until golden brown and cooked through.

Makes 8

puff pastry sausage rolls

see variations page 63

Many of us keep sheets of puff pastry in the freezer. These sausage rolls – *saucijzenbroodjes* – were made using 13cm (5in) square sheets. If these are not available, cut the squares from larger sheets. They pair well with onion chutney.

250g (9oz) minced beef
250g (9oz) minced pork
handful of finely chopped fresh parsley
¼ tsp ground white pepper
2 tsp flaky sea salt
¼ tsp ground nutmeg
2 eggs, beaten
75g (2¾oz) dried or panko breadcrumbs
10 x puff pastry squares (13 x 13cm/5 x 5in)

Combine the meats, parsley and spices together with a quarter of the beaten egg and all the breadcrumbs. Divide into 10 equal pieces and roll each piece into a small log.

Lay a sausage log on a puff pastry sheet, to the right of the centre, and brush the pastry on the right-hand side with a little of the remaining egg. Fold the left side of the pastry sheet over the meat to meet the edge of the right side. Use the tines of a fork to press down all three of the open sides. Brush the top with the remaining egg. Repeat with the remaining sausage and pastry sheets. Line a baking sheet with baking parchment and place the sausage rolls on the sheet. Keep them refrigerated while the oven preheats to 200°C (425°F). Bake the rolls for about 20 minutes until golden brown and cooked through.

Makes 10

GF Use gluten-free pastry and breadcrumbs.

herring salad

see variations page 64

Each spring, the herring season starts with the auctioning of the first keg of matjes herring. We eat it raw, by the tail, with onions or on a bun. Herring is also delicious in salads such as the *haringsalade*, served with buttered toast.

4 herrings (approx. 400g/14oz in total)
4 large, boiled potatoes, diced
2 tbsp crème fraîche
1 tbsp mayonnaise
1 tsp yellow or stoneground mustard
1 tbsp white wine vinegar
1 small shallot, sliced
1 small red apple
handful of chopped fresh chives, plus extra for garnish
1 small butterhead lettuce

Slice the herring into bite-sized pieces and mix with the potatoes.

Mix together the crème fraîche, mayonnaise and mustard and set aside. Sprinkle the vinegar over the shallot slices and let sit for 5 minutes, then drain. Core and dice the apple. Fold the onions into the potato and herring with a handful of chopped chives and the diced apple. Lastly, fold in the dressing.

Wash and dry the lettuce. Divide the leaves between four plates then divide the salad between them. Sprinkle with a little more of the fresh chives.

Serves 4

GF Use gluten-free mustard.

shrimp cocktail

see variations page 65

This cocktail (*garnalencocktail*) is such a 1970s classic but remains popular even today. The dressing is the perfect accompaniment to the traditional brown shrimp.

4 tbsp double cream
4 tbsp mayonnaise
2 tbsp tomato ketchup
1 tsp lemon juice
2 tbsp whisky, cognac or brandy (optional)
1 small butterhead lettuce
450g (1lb) cooked brown shrimp
pinch of paprika or cayenne pepper

Whip the double cream for about 1 minute until slightly thickened, by hand or using an electric whisk. Fold in the mayonnaise, ketchup, lemon juice and cognac or brandy, if using.

Carefully strip 4 leaves off the lettuce, and wash and dry them. Line 4 glasses or cups with the lettuce leaves and divide the shrimp among them. Dress the shrimp with the sauce and dust lightly with the paprika or cayenne. Refrigerate until ready to serve.

Serves 4

GF

belgian endive salad

see variations page 66

A delicious *witlofsalade* made from crisp Belgian endives usually appears around Easter and stays on the menu until autumn. It makes a great side salad, or a complete lunch if served with grilled chicken. In the winter, Belgian endive is most often used in casseroles (see page 144). Serve with bread and butter, cold cuts and gherkins.

400g (14oz) Belgian endive
4 tbsp olive or sunflower oil
2 tbsp white wine vinegar
1 tbsp Dijon mustard
2 tsp honey
salt and freshly ground black pepper

Cut the endives in half lengthways and remove the hard core at the bottom. Slice into half-moons, then quickly rinse under running water and leave to drain in a colander.

Whisk together the oil, vinegar, mustard and honey in a small bowl to create a vinaigrette.

Dress the endives just before serving and finish with a sprinkle of salt and pepper.

Serves 4

GF Use gluten-free mustard. **V Veg** See variations.

cucumber salad

see variations page 67

A cucumber salad (*komkommersalade*) is so refreshing, and open to many variations (see page 67). Serve with bread and butter.

2 large cucumbers
4 tbsp olive or sunflower oil
2 tbsp white wine vinegar
1 tsp granulated sugar
1 small shallot, finely chopped
1 tbsp finely chopped chives
½ tsp salt

Peel and slice the cucumbers. Place the slices on a deep plate or in a colander and sprinkle with the salt. Let rest for 10 minutes, as the salt removes some of the moisture from the cucumber. Drain the liquid.

Combine the oil, vinegar and sugar to create a sweet vinaigrette, then stir in the shallot. Carefully toss the cucumbers with the vinaigrette. Leave to chill in the fridge for 15 minutes, then serve cold sprinkled with the chives.

Serves 4

GF V Veg

salmon salad

see variations page 68

This salmon salad – *zalmsalade* – is considered a full meal salad. It can be served in individual portions, served with toast, or on a large platter so that people can help themselves. For a lighter dressing, substitute half of the mayonnaise for yoghurt.

1 x 418g (15oz) tin red or pink salmon
1 small cucumber
1 x 200g (7oz) tin peas and carrots, drained
1 tbsp capers
1 small shallot, chopped
5 tbsp mayonnaise
1 tbsp tomato ketchup
1 tsp chopped fresh dill
salt and freshly ground black pepper

Drain the salmon but retain the liquid and pass it through a fine sieve. Pick through the salmon and discard any bones and skin. Wash and dice half of the cucumber but do not peel.

In a bowl, combine the peas and carrots, capers, diced cucumber, shallots, 2 tablespoons of the mayonnaise and 2 tablespoons of the salmon liquid. Add a pinch of salt and fresh dill. Fold in the salmon, making sure to leave it in big chunks.

In a separate bowl, add the remainder of the mayonnaise, the tomato ketchup and 1 tablespoon of the salmon liquid. Mix to create a smooth dressing.

On a serving platter, make a small mound of the salad and cover it with the dressing. Slice the other half of the cucumber and layer the slices all around the salad. Sprinkle the remaining dill over the cucumber. Refrigerate for 30 minutes and serve chilled.

Serves 4 **GF**

potato salad

see variations page 69

The Dutch love potatoes in any way, shape or form. This salad (*aardappelsalade*) is a family staple in the summertime. It can be served as a side salad, a full meal salad or as a sandwich filling between two slices of buttered wholemeal bread.

4 eggs
500g (1lb 2oz) waxy potatoes, boiled and cooled
1 tbsp capers
75g (2¾oz) fresh or frozen peas, cooked
1 small shallot, finely chopped
3 tbsp mayonnaise
2 tbsp cider vinegar
handful of chopped fresh herbs, such as parsley, dill, chives, watercress
salt and freshly ground black pepper

Boil the eggs for 8 minutes, then leave to cool.

Dice the boiled and cold potatoes and add to a bowl. Fold in the capers, frozen peas and shallots. Peel the eggs, then dice and add them to the bowl.

Combine the mayonnaise and vinegar to create a light dressing. Add a pinch of salt and pepper, then add the dressing to the potato salad and mix through gently.

Fold the chopped herbs into the potato salad just before serving.

Serves 4

GF V

tomato soup with meatballs

see variations page 70

A classic recipe for a *tomatensoep* – a homemade tomato soup that will bring summer to your plate. Serve with a side of bread and butter.

1 tbsp butter
1 small onion, sliced
1 large carrot, diced
1kg (2lb 3oz) fresh ripe or tinned tomatoes, roughly chopped
2 vegetable or beef stock cubes
1 sprig of fresh thyme
250g (9oz) minced beef
salt and freshly ground black pepper

Melt the butter in a stock pot over a medium-high heat and sauté the onions until translucent, about 5 minutes. Add the carrots and tomatoes and cook for another 5 minutes, stirring constantly. Add 1 litre (1¾ pints) water, the stock cubes and thyme, bring to the boil, then reduce the heat and simmer, covered, for 20 minutes.

Season the minced beef with salt and pepper and knead well for a few minutes, until the meat comes together. Roll it into small meatballs (about the size of large marbles).

Remove the thyme sprig from the pan, then use a stick blender to blend the soup until smooth. Taste and season with salt, if needed. Stir the meatballs into the soup and let it simmer for another 15 minutes until the meatballs are cooked through.

Serves 4

GF Use gluten-free stock cubes.

brown bean soup

see variations page 71

Brown beans are a typical Dutch legume. If you can't find them to make this sturdy winter soup (*bruine bonensoep*) that is delicious and warming during cold evenings, you can use small red beans or pinto beans. Serve with wholemeal bread.

250g (9oz) dried brown beans or pinto beans
3 cloves
1 small onion
1 bay leaf
250g (9oz) mixed vegetables, such as leeks, celeriac, carrot, celery, parsley, green cabbage
1 beef or vegetable stock cube
300g (10½oz) smoked rope sausage
salt and freshly ground black pepper

Wash and rinse the beans, then soak them in water overnight. Rinse again and add the beans to a stock pot with enough water to cover. Stick the cloves into the onion and add to the pan along with the bay leaf. Cover, bring to the boil, then reduce the heat and cook the beans until tender, about 1 hour.

Discard the onion, cloves and bay leaf, and set two cupfuls of the cooked beans aside. Purée the remaining cooked beans using a blender or stick blender – if the liquid is too thick, add a little extra water. Add the chopped vegetables and the stock cube to the puréed beans and simmer until the vegetables are cooked, about 30 minutes. During the last 15 minutes of cooking time, add the reserved beans and the whole sausage and let it simmer in the soup. Remove the sausage, slice it and return to the pan before serving. Taste the soup and season with salt and pepper if desired.

Serves 4

GF Use a gluten-free sausage and stock cube.
V Use a vegetarian sausage and stock cube.
Veg Use a vegan sausage and stock cube.

chicken soup

see variations page 72

A classic soup for Sundays at Grandma's house – it has all the flavours of childhood. *Kippensoep* is best left to simmer on the back burner and enjoyed with bread and butter.

1 large chicken, about 2–2.5kg (4lb 4oz–5lb 8oz)
1 large onion, chopped
4 celery sticks, sliced, and leaves set aside
2 large carrots, diced
1 large tomato
5 sprigs of fresh parsley
2 bay leaves
pinch of dried thyme
10 black peppercorns
75g (2¾oz) vermicelli
salt

Place the chicken in a large stock pot with 2.5 litres (4½ pints) water and add half the onion, celery and carrots and the whole tomato. Strip the leaves off the parsley sprigs and set aside. Add the bare stems and the rest of the herbs and spices. Cover and allow to simmer for 2 hours, removing any surface scum every now and then.

Dampen paper towels and wring out the water. Use the towels to line a colander set over a clean stock pot and carefully ladle the liquid into the colander. Pick all the meat off the chicken and set aside. Discard the bones and the cooked vegetables.

Add the remainder of the fresh vegetables to the strained stock, bring to the boil, then reduce the heat and simmer uncovered until reduced by about 10 per cent – this should take about 15 minutes on a low heat.

Chop the chicken meat into bite-sized pieces and add to the hot soup, together with the vermicelli, 15 minutes before the end of the cooking time. Just before serving, stir in the parsley and celery leaves. Taste, and season with salt if needed.

Serves 4

GF Use gluten-free pasta.

split pea soup

see variations page 73

This stick-to-your-ribs soup was added to the list of Dutch cultural heritage dishes in 2019. As soon as the temperature drops below freezing, split pea soup (*snert*) is on the menu! A smoked rope sausage is traditional, but the soup can be enhanced with additional meat – see the variations on page 73.

400g (14oz) split peas
1 bay leaf
4 celery sticks or 150g (5¼oz) celeriac, roughly chopped (keep the celery leaves for garnish, if desired)
2 leeks, white part only, sliced
1 medium carrot, diced
1 smoked rope sausage
salt and freshly ground black pepper

Rinse the split peas in abundant water, then add them to 1.5 litres (1¾ pints) water in a large stock pot. Add the bay leaf, celery or celeriac, leeks and carrot. Bring to the boil, cover, then reduce the heat and let simmer for 30–40 minutes, or until the peas and the vegetables are soft. Add the smoked sausage 15 minutes before the end of the cooking time.

Remove one cup of cooked peas and the sausage, discard the bay leaf, and purée the remaining peas with a blender or stick blender. Stir the whole peas back into the soup. Slice the sausage into bite-size pieces and stir back into the soup. Taste and season with salt and freshly ground black pepper, and garnish with celery leaves, if using.

Serves 4

GF Use a gluten-free sausage.
V Use a vegetarian sausage.
Veg Use a vegan sausage.

vegetable soup

see variations page 74

Vegetable soup is welcome every day of the week. On Sundays, *groentensoep* traditionally consisted of thinly sliced vegetables and a clearer stock; during weekdays it was a savoury mix of chunky vegetables. It's a quick soup to make in any season.

3 vegetable or beef stock cubes
1 tbsp butter or non-dairy spread
1 leek, cut into half moons
1 small onion, diced
2 medium carrots, diced
2 celery sticks, chopped, and leaves set aside
300g (10½oz) mixed vegetables, such as cauliflower, cabbage, celeriac, broccoli, tomatoes, green beans
salt

Bring 1.5 litres (1¾ pints) water to a simmer in a large stock pot. Stir in the stock cubes.

Melt the butter in a frying pan and sauté the leeks, onions, carrots and celery until translucent, 5–6 minutes. Transfer to the stock pot.

Chop the mixed vegetables into bite-sized pieces and add all except the broccoli to the stock pot. Simmer for 20 minutes, or until soft, adding the broccoli for the last 5 minutes of the cooking time. Taste, and season with salt if needed. Stir in the celery leaves just before serving.

Serves 4

GF Use gluten-free stock cubes.
V Veg Use non-dairy spread.

lentil soup

see variations page 75

Linzensoep was traditionally the choice of young students off to college: it was easy to make and affordable. Nowadays, it offers a great base dish from which to expand. Serve with plenty of buttered bread.

350g (12½oz) brown lentils
1 tbsp vegetable oil
1 large carrot, diced
1 leek, halved and sliced into half moons
1 onion
3 garlic cloves, chopped
100g (3½oz) tomato purée
3 vegetable stock cubes
1 bay leaf
salt

Wash and rinse the lentils, then add them to a stock pot with 1.5 litres (1¾ pints) water.

Heat the oil in a pan, then cook the carrots, leeks, onions and garlic until fragrant and transparent, about 10 minutes, stirring frequently. Add the tomato purée and stir for 2 more minutes, then add to the stock pot.

Add the stock cubes and bay leaf to the stock pot and let it simmer for 30 minutes, or until the lentils are cooked through. Taste and add salt if needed.

Serves 4

GF Use gluten-free stock cubes. **V Veg**

mushroom soup

see variations page 76

In the provinces of Limburg, North Brabant and Gelderland, where mushrooms are traditionally grown, *champignonsoep* is a frequent choice. Serve with sliced wholemeal bread.

2 vegetable or chicken stock cubes
2 tbsp butter
500g (1lb 2oz) button mushrooms, sliced
1 small onion, diced
2 celery sticks, sliced
30g (1oz) plain flour
pinch of dried thyme
3 sprigs of fresh parsley, leaves stripped and stems chopped
125ml (4½fl oz) double cream
salt

Bring 1.25 litres (1¾ pints) water to a simmer in a large stock pot. Stir in the stock cubes.

Melt the butter in a frying pan and sauté the mushrooms, onion and celery until soft, about 5 to 6 minutes. Set aside a quarter of the sautéed vegetables.

Sprinkle the flour over the vegetables still in the pan and stir until they are coated. Now stir in ladlefuls of the stock, one at a time, to make a thick soup, making sure the liquid has been absorbed into the soup before adding more. Add the thyme and parsley stems and simmer, over a low heat, for about 15 minutes.

Add the double cream, taste, and add salt if needed. Stir through the remaining vegetables and sprinkle the parsley leaves over before serving.

Serves 4

GF Use gluten-free stock cubes and flour.
V Use vegetable stock cubes. **Veg** Use vegetable stock cubes and non-dairy cream.

mustard soup

see variations page 77

The key to success with *mosterdsoep* is to use a good-quality coarse grain mustard.

200g (7oz) bacon lardons
2 tbsp butter
1 leek, halved and chopped into half moons
2 tbsp plain flour
1 litre (1¾ pints) chicken or vegetable stock
75ml (2¾fl oz) double cream
3 tbsp coarse grain mustard

Fry the lardons in a stock pot for 10 minutes over a medium heat. Remove from the pan and set aside.

Melt the butter in the same pan and fry the leeks for about 5 minutes, until translucent. Sprinkle the flour over the leeks and stir until it all comes together. Slowly add the stock, a ladleful at a time, stirring constantly so that the liquid is absorbed, about 5 minutes, then simmer for 10 minutes over a low heat, stirring every now and then.

Right before serving, stir in the double cream and the mustard. Top with the lardons, and serve.

Serves 4

GF Use gluten-free flour, stock and mustard.

variations

fried eggs on bread

see base recipe page 15

fried eggs with roast beef & horseradish
Omit the ham. Spread 1 tsp horseradish on top of the butter, then layer each slice of bread with a slice of roast beef and cheese before adding the fried eggs. **GF**

fried eggs with smoked turkey & tomatoes
Omit the ham. Cut the tomato into thin rounds. Place a slice of smoked turkey, the cheese and slices of fresh tomato on each buttered slice of bread before adding the fried eggs. **GF**

fried eggs with bacon & roasted tomato
Omit the ham. Fry 4 rashers of bacon until crispy and layer them on top of the buttered bread. Cut the tomato in half horizontally and cook them, cut-side down, in the hot bacon fat for 3–4 minutes until slightly roasted and soft. Top the bacon with the egg and finish with the cheese. Season the tomato and serve on the side. **GF**

fried eggs with red pepper & onions
Omit the ham. Slice 1 small onion, the tomato and a deseeded red pepper into strips and quickly sauté them in 1 tbsp olive oil until soft, 5–6 minutes. Season with salt and pepper. Add the cheese slices to the buttered bread, top with the tomato mix and place the eggs on top. **GF V**

GF Use gluten-free bread.

variations

devilled eggs

see base recipe page 16

curried devilled eggs
Prepare as directed, substituting ½ tsp curry powder for the mustard. Top with 1 tbsp chopped fresh coriander instead of the chives and cayenne pepper. **GF V**

peanut & chilli devilled eggs
Omit the butter, mustard, chives and cayenne pepper. Mix 2 tsp unsalted peanut butter and 1 tsp sweet chilli sauce into the egg yolks. Top with a drizzle of sweet chilli sauce. **GF V**

devilled eggs with prawns
Add 50g (1¾oz) small cooked and peeled prawns and a pinch of season-all seasoning to the egg yolks. Top each filled egg with a single prawn or 1 tsp caviar. Omit the chives and cayenne pepper. **GF**

devilled eggs with anchovies & capers
Omit the salt and the chives. Chop 1 tsp capers, and set 8 capers aside for the garnish. Drain a 50g (1¾oz) tin of anchovies and cut the fillets in half. Set 8 pieces aside for the garnish. Mash 2 anchovy halves with the egg yolk, butter, chopped capers and pepper and use to fill the egg halves. Decorate each half with a piece of anchovy and a caper. **GF**

GF Use gluten-free mustard.

variations

savoury tart

see base recipe page 19

three-cheese tart

Omit broccoli and ham. Grate 50g (1¾oz) blue cheese and 75g (2¾oz) mild Cheddar over the base. Beat the eggs and cream with 2 tbsp fresh chives and the mature Cheddar. Bake. **GF V**

salmon & red pepper tart

Omit the broccoli and ham. Replace the cheese with 150g (5¼oz) garlic and herb soft cheese. Distribute a 400g (14oz) tin of salmon, 1 sliced red pepper and half the cheese over the base. Beat the eggs and cream with the rest of the cheese and bake as directed. **GF**

spinach & walnut tart

Omit the broccoli and ham. Replace the cheese with 150g (5¼oz) garlic and herb soft cheese. Sauté 1 chopped shallot in 1 tbsp butter. Add 200g (7oz) spinach and cook until wilted. Distribute the spinach, half the cheese and 50g (1¾oz) chopped walnuts over the base. Beat the eggs and cream with the rest of the cheese and bake as directed. **GF V**

leek & bacon tart

Make the spinach and walnut tart (above), but replace shallot with 150g (5¼oz) bacon, fried until brown. Remove from pan and fry chopped whites of 3 leeks. Add splash of water, cover, simmer for 5 minutes. Sprinkle base with 2 tbsp fresh breadcrumbs (gluten-free if required), leeks, bacon and half the cheese. Beat eggs and cream with rest of cheese. Bake. **GF**

GF Use gluten-free pastry.

variations

flour porridge

see base recipe page 20

lamb's porridge
Omit the flour. Place a Dutch rusk or piece of dry toast into a deep bowl. Combine the milk, lemon zest and salt in a pan and bring to a boil. Pour the hot milk over the rusk. Sprinkle 1 tsp sugar on top and break the rusk into bite-sized pieces with a spoon. **GF V Veg**

beer flour porridge
Omit the lemon zest and cook as directed. Add a small splash of brown ale to the porridge just before serving. **GF V Veg**

wholemeal flour porridge
Replace the white flour with the same amount of wholemeal flour and cook as directed. Add 1–2 tbsp wheat bran to the finished porridge, if desired. **V Veg**

buttermilk flour porridge with sultanas
Replace the milk with buttermilk and omit the lemon zest. Mix the flour into the milk before bringing it up to a simmer – do not boil as it may curdle. Stir in 80g (3oz) sultanas and allow to simmer for 5 minutes. Sprinkle with a pinch of cinnamon or nutmeg. **GF V Veg**

cinnamon flour porridge
Replace the lemon zest with a cinnamon stick and cook as directed. **GF V Veg**

GF Use gluten-free flour. Veg Use non-dairy milk and buttermilk.

variations

beef croquettes

see base recipe page 22

goulash croquettes
Omit the parsley and thyme. Make the sauce with the flour, butter and stock. Add 50g (1¾oz) chopped roasted red peppers, 1 tsp paprika, 1 tsp tomato purée, ½ chopped shallot and 2 crushed garlic cloves with the meat and simmer until the peppers are tender. **GF**

chicken satay croquettes
Replace the meat with 200g (7oz) chicken and omit the thyme and parsley. Make the sauce with the flour, butter and stock. Add 50g (1¾oz) unsweetened peanut butter, 1 small diced red chilli, 1 crushed garlic clove, a pinch of ground ginger, 2 tbsp coconut milk, 1 tbsp sweet soy sauce (kecap manis) and a squeeze of lemon juice and simmer until thick. **GF**

cheese croquettes
Substitute the same quantity of milk for the stock and white pepper for black. Replace the meat with 175g (6oz) grated mature Cheddar, Gouda or a mix of Cheddar and blue cheese. Add to the sauce and cook for 4 minutes, stirring, until melted. **GF V**

mixed vegetable croquettes
Substitute 200g (7oz) chopped cooked vegetables for the meat; add a pinch of nutmeg. **GF V**

GF Use gluten-free flour and breadcrumbs.

variations

omelette

see base recipe page 24

ham & cheese omelette

Top the omelette with 40g (1½oz) grated mature cheese and 2 slices ham. Fold the omelette, turn down the heat, cover, and cook for 2 minutes, or until the cheese has melted. **GF**

brie & salami omelette

Place 4 slices salami and 2 slices Brie on one half of the omelette. Fold the omelette, turn down the heat, cover, and cook for 2 more minutes, or until the Brie has slightly melted. **GF**

fresh herb & feta omelette

Sauté 2 tbsp chopped onion in a sprinkle of olive oil until translucent, then add salt, pepper and 40g (1½oz) mixed herbs and leafy greens, and cook until wilted. Place the greens on one half of the omelette. Crumble 20g (¾oz) feta cheese over the greens, fold over the omelette, turn down the heat, cover, and cook for 2 more minutes. **GF V**

spinach & tomato omelette

Cut 100g (3½oz) cherry tomatoes in half and chop 50g (1¾oz) fresh spinach. Sauté 2 tbsp chopped onion in 1 tbsp butter until translucent, about 3 minutes. Add the tomatoes and spinach and stir once or twice. Pour the eggs over the vegetables and cook the omelette as directed. When the top is almost cooked through, sprinkle 25g (¾oz) grated cheese on top, cover, and cook for 2 more minutes until the cheese has melted. **GF V**

GF Use gluten-free bread.

variations

chicken vol-au-vents

see base recipe page 25

chicken curry vol-au-vents
Add 2 heaped tbsp curry powder to the finished sauce.

prawn vol-au-vents
Omit the chicken. Replace the chicken stock with 700ml (25fl oz) fish or seafood stock. Fold 250g (9oz) cooked and peeled prawns into the finished sauce and sprinkle the filled vol-au-vents with fresh dill instead of parsley.

mushroom vol-au-vents
Omit the chicken and increase the quantity of mushrooms to 650g (1lb 7oz) and the butter to 50g (1¾oz). Replace the chicken stock with 700ml (25fl oz) vegetable stock. **V**

egg & caper vol-au-vents
Omit the chicken, mushrooms and wine. Make the sauce with the butter, flour and 700ml (25fl oz) vegetable stock. Boil 6 eggs for 8 minutes, leave to cool, peel then chop and fold them into the sauce. Add 1 heaped tbsp capers and 1 tsp coarse ground mustard to the sauce. Sprinkle the filled vol-au-vents with 1 tbsp fresh parsley leaves. **V**

variations

sausage bread rolls

see base recipe page 26

cheese & sausage bread rolls
Omit the parsley. Mix 100g (3½oz) grated mature Cheddar with the mince, before rolling it into small logs, and cook as directed.

spinach, sun-dried tomato & sausage bread rolls
Omit the parsley. Chop 50g (1¾oz) fresh spinach and 50g (1¾oz) sun-dried tomatoes into small pieces and mix into the meat before rolling it into small logs. Cook as directed.

caramelised onion & sausage bread rolls
Use 2 tbsp butter or oil to caramelise 1 small sliced onion over a low heat until golden brown, about 20 minutes. Cool, chop and fold the onions into the meat mixture before rolling it into small logs. Cook as directed.

bacon, mustard & sausage bread rolls
Roll a slice of streaky bacon around each sausage log and brush with yellow or stoneground mustard before rolling it in the dough. Cook as directed.

variations

puff pastry sausage rolls

see base recipe page 29

puff pastry ham & cheese rolls
Reduce the minced beef and pork to 200g (7oz) each. Chop 50g (1¾oz) cooked ham and 50g (1¾oz) mature Cheddar into small cubes and mix them into the meat filling. Cook as directed. **GF**

spicy puff pastry sausage rolls
Omit the nutmeg and the parsley. Add 2 tbsp sweet chilli sauce to the meat filling. If you like it spicier, brush 1 tsp chilli sauce onto the pastry sheets beneath where the meat will be placed. **GF**

puff pastry mushroom & sausage rolls
Add 75g (2¾oz) chopped mushrooms, sautéed in 1 tbsp butter or vegetable oil to the meat filling. Substitute a pinch of dried thyme for the nutmeg and cook as directed. **GF**

puff pastry cheese & sausage rolls
Cut 250g (9oz) mature Cheddar into 10 equal strips (if you prefer a milder cheese, use mozzarella). Wrap the meat filling around each strip of cheese before adding to the puff pastry sheets. Cook as directed. **GF**

GF Use gluten-free flour, pastry and breadcrumbs.

variations

herring salad

see base recipe page 30

herring salad with beetroot & gherkins
Omit the vinegar and shallot. Add 250g (9oz) diced cooked beetroot to the salad with 100g (3½oz) diced gherkins and a splash of the gherkin juice. Refrigerate for 3 hours before serving. **GF**

herring salad with horseradish & dill
Make the salad as directed, replacing the mustard with horseradish and the chives with fresh dill. Omit the apple. **GF**

herring salad with tomatoes & avocado
Omit the apple. Add 100g (3½oz) halved cherry tomatoes and the cubed flesh of 1 avocado to the salad. **GF**

herring salad with celery & egg
Slice 2 large celery sticks into half-moons. Boil 2 eggs for 8 minutes, then leave to cool slightly, peel and cut in half lengthways. Remove the egg yolks and mash them with a fork, then mix them into the dressing. Cut the egg whites into bite-sized pieces and fold into the salad with the celery. **GF**

GF Use gluten-free mustard.

variations

shrimp cocktail

see base recipe page 33

shrimp cocktail with grapes & walnuts
Slice 10 white seedless grapes in half lengthways. Lightly toast 50g (1¾oz) walnuts in a dry frying pan over a medium heat for 2–3 minutes. Chop the walnuts into small pieces and toss with the grapes, 350g (12½oz) of the shrimp and 1 tbsp of the sauce. Set on top of the lettuce, dress with the remaining sauce and shrimp. Dust with paprika or cayenne. **GF**

shrimp cocktail with avocado & lime
Omit the lettuce. Cut 2 avocados in half and remove the stones. Brush the flesh with lime juice. Toss the shrimp with the sauce and fill the avocado halves with a generous serving of shrimp. Dust with paprika or cayenne and serve with a wedge of lime. **GF**

shrimp cocktail with tomato & cucumber
Omit the sauce and paprika. Toss the shrimp with 2 diced and deseeded tomatoes and half a diced (unpeeled) cucumber. Whisk together 4 tbsp olive oil, 2 tbsp white wine vinegar, 1 tbsp chopped fresh parsley, ½ tsp yellow or stoneground mustard (gluten-free if required) and a pinch of salt and pepper. Use to dress the salad and place on top of the lettuce leaves. **GF**

shrimp & grapefruit cocktail
Peel and segment 1 large grapefruit, removing the papery skin of each wedge to reveal the flesh. Place 4 slices of grapefruit on top of each bed of lettuce and place the shrimp cocktail on top. Dust with paprika or cayenne. **GF**

variations

belgian endive salad

see base recipe page 34

belgian endive salad with apples & eggs
Core and slice 1 sweet red apple into thin wedges. Boil 2 eggs for 8 minutes, then leave to cool. Peel the eggs, then slice into four wedges each. Alternate the apple and egg wedges along the side of the salad before serving. **GF V**

creamy belgian endive salad with dill & chicken
Double the quantity of ingredients in the vinaigrette, but replace the mustard with mayonnaise and omit the honey. Chop a handful of fresh dill fronds and mix into the vinaigrette along with a pinch of salt. Cut 400g (14oz) cold cooked chicken into bite-sized pieces and scatter over the chopped endive. Dress with dill vinaigrette just before serving. **GF**

belgian endive salad with mandarins & smoked almonds
Drain a 200g (7oz) tin of mandarin segments, retaining the juice. Replace the honey in the vinaigrette with the juice and use ½ tbsp mustard. Mix the mandarin segments with the chopped endive and scatter over 75g (2¾oz) smoked almonds just before serving. **GF V Veg**

belgian endive salad with prawns, potatoes & red grapefruit
Add 350g (12½oz) cooked and peeled small prawns, 2 boiled and diced potatoes, and the segments of 1 red grapefruit to a bowl. Toss with the sliced endive to combine. Double the quantity of ingredients in the vinaigrette and dress just before serving. **GF**

GF Use gluten-free mustard.

variations

cucumber salad

see base recipe page 37

cucumber salad with mirin & ginger

Replace the white wine vinegar and sugar with 2 tbsp mirin. Peel a 3cm (1¼in) piece of fresh root ginger and cut into thin matchsticks. Mix both with the cucumber, and chill before serving. **GF V Veg**

cucumber salad with red chillies

Make the cucumber salad with mirin and ginger (above). Slice 2 small red chillies into rings and toss through the salad. **GF V Veg**

cucumber salad with italian herbs

Add a pinch of Italian dried herbs (or 1 tbsp mixed fresh herbs such as oregano, thyme, basil, parsley) to the cucumber salad. If using fresh basil, do not refrigerate – sprinkle over the salad just before serving. **GF V Veg**

cucumber, tomato & onion salad

Halve 125g (4½oz) cherry tomatoes. Replace the shallot with 1 small onion, sliced. Pickle the onion slices in the vinegar and sugar for 30 minutes, then use the vinegar to make the vinaigrette, and fold the cherry tomatoes and pickled onion slices into the salad. **GF V Veg**

variations

salmon salad

see base recipe page 38

salmon & egg salad
Boil 3 eggs for 8 minutes, then leave to cool. Peel the eggs, then dice one and fold it into the salad, together with 1 tsp yellow or stoneground mustard (optional, gluten-free if required). Slice the remaining 2 eggs and alternate with the slices of cucumber around the salad. **GF**

spinach, salmon & tomato salad
Chop 50g (1¾oz) salad leaves and fold into the salad. Use another 100g (3½oz) leaves as a bed on which to serve the salad. Halve 250g (9oz) cherry tomatoes. Add half the tomatoes to the salad and use the other half to decorate around the salad with the cucumber slices. **GF**

potato, olive & salmon salad with vinaigrette
Omit the mayonnaise and ketchup. Roughly chop 2 boiled waxy potatoes and 75g (2¾oz) pitted black olives and fold them into the salad. Make a vinaigrette: whisk together 3 tbsp olive or sunflower oil, 1½ tbsp white wine vinegar, ½ tbsp yellow or stoneground mustard (gluten-free if required) and the fresh dill, and dress the salad just before serving. Finish with a sprinkle of salt and black pepper. **GF**

avocado, tomato, salmon & rocket salad
Add 1 peeled and diced avocado, 50g (1¾oz) rocket and 125g (4½oz) halved cherry tomatoes to the salad. Mix carefully to combine and serve chilled. **GF**

variations

potato salad

see base recipe page 41

potato salad with apples & gherkins
Add 1 large sweet red apple, cored and diced, and 2 chopped gherkins to the salad. Replace the vinegar in the dressing with juice from the gherkin jar. **GF V**

potato salad with a dill & yoghurt dressing
Prepare the salad as directed. Replace 2 tbsp mayonnaise with Greek yoghurt. Fold a handful of chopped fresh dill into the dressing. **GF V**

potato salad with bacon & onions
Omit the mayonnaise, capers and eggs. Replace the shallot with a diced onion. Slice 250g (9oz) streaky bacon into thin strips and fry until the fat is translucent and the bacon begins to brown and crisp, 6–7 minutes. Set aside. Sauté the onions in the bacon fat until translucent, 5–6 minutes. Combine the onions and bacon with the potatoes and peas. Increase the cider vinegar to 4 tbsp and add to the bacon fat. Bring to the boil and stir a couple of times to loosen the pan juices, then cook for 2 minutes over a high heat. Pour the hot vinegar over the potato mix and fold it in. Serve warm. **GF**

limburger cold salad (*koude schotel*)
Dice 600g (1lb 5oz) cold cooked meat (leftovers from a roast are ideal). Combine with the apples & gherkins salad recipe (above) and double the quantity of dressing. This salad is best made the day before it is eaten so that the flavours can blend. **GF**

variations

tomato soup with meatballs

see base recipe page 42

tomato soup with vermicelli & chopped tomatoes

Omit the meatballs and use vegetable stock cubes and 1 tbsp olive oil instead of butter. Set aside 2 tbsp of the chopped tomatoes. Simmer the soup for 20 minutes, stirring 75g (2¾oz) uncooked vermicelli (gluten-free if required) into the soup 10 minutes before the end of the cooking time. Toss the extra chopped tomatoes with a pinch of salt and pepper and use to top the soup. **GF V Veg**

tomato soup with ginger & bean sprouts

Omit the meatballs and use only vegetable stock cubes and 1 tbsp olive oil instead of butter. Add 2 tbsp julienned fresh root ginger, 2 tsp ground ginger, 1 tbsp granulated sugar and 1 tbsp rice wine vinegar to the soup and simmer for 20 minutes. Stir in 200g (7oz) fresh bean sprouts just before serving. **GF V Veg**

italian tomato soup with meatballs & croutons

Add 1 tsp each of dried oregano and basil to the soup 5 minutes before the end of the cooking time. Serve each bowl with a handful of croutons (gluten-free if required). **GF**

tomato soup with meatballs, cream & basil

Top each bowl of finished soup with strips of fresh basil, a sprinkling of black pepper and 1 tbsp double cream. **GF**

GF Use gluten-free stock cubes.

variations

brown bean soup

see base recipe page 45

brown bean soup with a bacon & leeks

Cook the soup as directed, omitting the sausage. Garnish with 150g (5¼oz) bacon lardons, fried until brown, and the sliced white of a small leek fried in the bacon fat until golden. **GF**

brown bean soup with portobello mushrooms

Cook the soup as directed, omitting the sausage and using vegetable stock. Fry 250g (9oz) chopped portobello mushrooms, 1 garlic clove, ½ tsp smoked paprika and a pinch of salt and pepper in 1 tbsp olive oil until softened. Stir into the cooked soup. **GF V Veg**

brown bean soup with a tomato & yoghurt topping

Cook the soup as directed, omitting the sausage and using vegetable stock. Garnish with 2 diced tomatoes (seeds removed) seasoned with salt and pepper and 100g (3½oz) plain Greek yoghurt (dairy-free if required) combined with 3 tbsp chopped parsley. **GF V Veg**

brown bean soup with ginger, celery & allspice

Omit the sausage and use vegetable stock. Add 4 allspice berries, 2 tsp ground ginger, 1 tbsp granulated sugar, 1 tbsp tomato purée, 2 diced celery sticks and 2 chopped garlic cloves to the soup when the beans are tender. Simmer for 30 minutes. Do not purée the beans. Remove the allspice berries and stir in a handful of chopped celery leaves just before serving. This dish is often served with chilli paste and boiled rice on the side. **GF V Veg**

GF Use a gluten-free stock cube.

variations

chicken soup

see base recipe page 46

chicken soup with meatballs & vegetables
Remove the breast fillets before cooking the chicken. Chop finely, season with salt and pepper and roll into small meatballs. Make the soup as directed, adding the meatballs and 250g (9oz) chopped mixed vegetables (such as green cabbage, leeks, cauliflower, celeriac) 30 minutes before the end of the cooking time. Simmer but do not boil. **GF**

chicken soup with fresh tomatoes & basil
Cook the soup as directed. Dice 3 tomatoes and toss with a pinch each of dried oregano, dried basil, salt and pepper. Add to the soup just before serving. Top with fresh basil. **GF**

chicken soup with ginger & lemongrass
Add 5cm (2in) root ginger and 2 stalks of lemongrass to the initial cooking. Discard with the rest of the vegetables. Purée 2cm (3/4in) root ginger with 2 garlic cloves, 1 shallot and 1/2 tsp turmeric. Fry in 1 tbsp rapeseed oil until it is fragrant, then add to the soup with the chicken. Season with salt. Top with a handful of fresh bean sprouts and a squeeze of lime juice. **GF**

chicken & chilli peanut soup
Replace the peppercorns with 4 pimento berries. Stir 3 heaped tbsp unsweetened peanut butter and a small red chilli into the stock with the vegetables. Omit the vermicelli. **GF**

GF Use gluten-free pasta.

variations

split pea soup

see base recipe page 48

split pea soup with smoked ham & potato

Omit the sausage if desired. Simmer a smoked ham hock with the vegetables. Remove the meat from the bones, dice and add back to the soup after pureéing the peas. Add 2 diced potatoes and simmer until the potatoes are cooked through, about 20 minutes. **GF**

split pea soup with pork ribs & fried leeks

Omit the sausage if desired. Add 500g (1lb 2oz) pork ribs to simmer with the peas. Remove the meat from the bones, dice and add back to the soup after pureéing the peas. Fry 1 sliced leek in 1 tbsp butter until golden, about 5 minutes, and stir in just before serving. **GF**

split pea soup with chorizo

Cook the soup as directed, omitting the sausage. Fry 4 chorizo sausages (250g/9oz in total) in 2 tbsp olive oil over a medium heat for 10 minutes. Save the flavoured oil. Slice the sausages and add to the soup. Sprinkle 1 tbsp flavoured oil over each serving. **GF**

split pea soup with fresh peas & mint

Omit the sausage. Stir in 150g (5¼oz) frozen fresh peas after puréeing the peas. Simmer again to cook the peas, about 10 minutes. Top the soup with a sprinkling of fresh mint and finish with a dollop of soured cream (for a vegan soup use non-dairy soured cream). **GF V Veg**

GF Use a gluten-free sausage and stock cube. V Use a vegetarian sausage and stock cube. Veg Use a vegan sausage and stock cube.

variations

vegetable soup

see base recipe page 49

vegetable soup with meatballs
Combine 250g (9oz) minced beef with a handful of finely chopped fresh parsley and season with salt and pepper. Roll the mixture into small meatballs, the size of marbles. Add to the soup with the mixed vegetables and simmer for 20 minutes. **GF**

creamed vegetable soup with fried onions
Use vegetable stock. After simmering the soup, purée it using a stick blender, adding a splash of milk or double cream (for a vegan soup use non-dairy milk or cream). Finely slice a small onion, toss with 2 heaped tbsp cornflour, and fry in rapeseed oil until golden, about 3 minutes. Drain on kitchen towel, sprinkle with salt and use to top the soup. **GF Veg V**

vegetable soup with pasta & tomatoes
Use vegetable stock. Add 75g (2¾oz) pasta shapes (gluten-free if required) to the soup, with 2 chopped and deseeded tomatoes, 10 minutes before end of the cooking time. **GF Veg V**

vegetable soup with savoy cabbage, red peppers & potatoes
Omit the mixed vegetables and use vegetable stock. Add 100g (3½oz) chopped Savoy cabbage, 2 sliced red peppers, 2 small diced potatoes, and ½ tsp caraway seeds. Simmer for 15 minutes. Pour 1 tbsp double cream (use non-dairy cream for a vegan soup) over each bowl before serving. **GF Veg V**

GF Use gluten-free stock cubes and pasta. Veg Use dairy-free spread.

variations

lentil soup

see base recipe page 51

chorizo & lentil soup

Fry 4 chorizo sausages (250g/9oz in total and gluten-free if required) in 2 tbsp olive oil over a medium heat for 10 minutes. Save the flavoured oil. Slice the sausages and add to the soup together with the stock cubes and the bay leaf. Sprinkle the flavoured oil over the soup before serving and top with a little freshly chopped coriander. **GF**

curried pumpkin & lentil soup

Toss 150g (5¼oz) cubed pumpkin with 1 tbsp curry powder and add to the soup, 15 minutes before the end of the cooking time **GF V Veg**

lentil soup with spinach & egg

Stir 150g (5¼oz) fresh spinach into the cooked soup and stir a few times until the leaves have wilted slightly. Boil 2 eggs for 8 minutes, then leave to cool. Peel the eggs, then slice and serve over the soup. **GF V**

lentil & chickpea soup with ras-el-hanout

Add 130g (4½oz) drained chickpeas and 1 tsp each of cumin, ras-el-hanout and smoked paprika. Top the soup with a small handful of chopped fresh coriander leaves and a dollop of yoghurt before serving. **GF V Veg**

GF Use gluten-free stock cubes.

variations

mushroom soup

see base recipe page 52

mushroom soup with sherry & prawns

Add 2 tbsp tomato purée and a splash of dry sherry to the finished soup with the parsley and thyme and simmer for 10 minutes. Add 150g (5¼oz) cooked and peeled small prawns to the soup 5 minutes before the end of the cooking time. **GF**

gratinated mushroom soup

Butter 4 pieces of bread, sprinkle with 50g (1¾oz) of grated aged Gouda cheese and cook under the grill until the cheese has melted. For a vegan soup use non-dairy cheese. Add one to each bowl or cup of soup. **GF Veg V**

mushroom soup with carrots & peas

Sauté 2 diced carrots with the onions, mushrooms and celery. Stir in 100g (3½oz) frozen or fresh peas before serving. **GF Veg V**

mixed mushroom soup

Use a variety of mushrooms, such as button, cremini and oyster for this soup. **GF Veg V**

GF Use gluten-free stock cubes, flour and bread.
Veg Use vegetable stock cubes and non-dairy cream. V Use vegetable stock cubes.

variations

mustard soup

see base recipe page 54

mustard soup with beer & sausages
Add 125ml (4½fl oz) bock beer, or dark beer, and 3 pork sausages (gluten-free if required) to the soup, after stirring in the stock. Cook as directed. Slice the sausages and return them to the soup before serving. **GF**

gratinated mustard soup with leyden cheese
Butter 4 pieces of bread (gluten-free if required), sprinkle with 50g (1¾oz) of grated Leyden (caraway) cheese and cook under the grill until the cheese has melted. Add one to each bowl or cup of soup. If you can't find caraway cheese, use your favourite cheese and add a pinch of caraway seeds to the bowl. **GF**

mussel & mustard soup
Add 150g (5¼oz) steamed mussels (see page 118) to the finished soup, bring to the boil and simmer for 2 more minutes before serving. **GF**

smoked salmon & mustard soup
Divide 120g (4¼oz) thinly sliced smoked salmon between the bowls of soup, just before serving. **GF**

GF Use gluten-free flour, stock and mustard.

family meals

On Sundays, many of us still gather around the table with friends and family. Traditionally, dinner consisted of soup, meat, potatoes and one vegetable, with a dairy-based dessert. Nowadays, many families skip the soup and turn to easy-to-make casseroles instead, or *stamppots* – mashed potatoes with vegetables. What stays the same is the pleasure of sharing a meal with loved ones.

curly endive stamppot

see variations page 119

Andijvie, better known as curly endive, frisée or just chicory, is similar to a head of lettuce, but with looser, narrower leaves with frilly tips. It has a slightly bitter taste. In this *stamppot* it is not cooked, but folded in just before serving, giving a satisfying freshness to the mashed potatoes.

1kg (2lb 3oz) floury potatoes (such as Desiree, King Edward, Maris Piper), quartered
1 head of curly endive (approx. 700g/1lb 8oz)
1 x 250g (9oz) smoked rope sausage
milk or butter, for mashing (optional)
salt and freshly ground black pepper

Put the potatoes in a pan with enough water to cover. Sprinkle 1 teaspoon of salt into the water, cover, and bring to the boil for 15 minutes. In the meantime, wash and chop the leaves of the endive, removing any wilted or brown leaves and discarding the bitter, tough stem end. Fold the leaves into a clean tea towel and give it a good shake to remove all the water. Add the sausage to the potatoes for the last 5 minutes of the cooking time.

Remove the sausage from the pan and set aside. Drain the potatoes, saving some of the water. Mash the potatoes until soft and fluffy. Adjust the seasoning to taste. If the *stamppot* is too dry, add 1 tablespoon of the drained cooking liquid at a time. If you prefer, you can also add a little milk or butter to make it richer. Chop the sausage and fold in with the chopped endive just before serving. Transfer the *stamppot* to a large platter or bowl.

Serves 4

GF Use a gluten-free sausage.
V Use a vegetarian sausage. **Veg** Use a vegan sausage.

apple & potato stamppot

see variations page 120

Officially known as *hete bliksem*, the nickname for this *stamppot* is 'hot lightning' because the juice in the apples retains all the heat, so beware! 'Hot lightning' pairs well with pork chops (see page 106) and onion gravy (see page 132).

1kg (2lb 3oz) floury potatoes (such as Desiree, King Edward, Maris Piper), quartered
250g (9oz) sweet apples (such as Gala)
250g (9oz) tart apples (such as Granny Smith, Braeburn)
1 bay leaf
2 cloves
milk or butter, for mashing (optional)
salt and freshly ground black pepper

Put the potatoes in a pan with enough water to cover: the pot should be big enough that the potatoes only fill it halfway. Sprinkle 1 teaspoon of salt into the pot, cover, and bring to the boil for 10 minutes. Peel and core the apples, cut them into quarters and stick the bay leaf and cloves into a piece of apple, so you'll be able to find them later. After 10 minutes, add the apples to the pan, cover, and continue to boil for a further 10 minutes.

Drain the potatoes, saving some of the water. Discard the cloves and the bay leaf. Mash the potatoes and the apples, adjusting the seasoning to taste. If the *stamppot* is too dry, add 1 tablespoon of the drained cooking liquid at a time. If you prefer, you can also add a little milk or butter to make it richer. Transfer the *stamppot* to a large platter or bowl.

Serves 4

GF V Veg Use non-dairy milk and butter.

carrot & onion hutspot

see variations page 121

A popular *stamppot* with children because of its sweetness, this carrot and onion dish is said to have been discovered in Leiden during the siege of 1574, when the Spanish left their dinner behind while running for the proverbial hills. It's also one of the few of this style of dish that is not referred to as *stamppot*, but as *hutspot* (hotchpotch). *Hutspot* is traditionally served with braised beef (*klapstuk)* (see page 96).

1kg (2lb 3oz) floury potatoes (such as Desiree, King Edward, Maris Piper), quartered
600g (1lb 5oz) carrots (preferably large winter carrots), cut to same size as potatoes
300g (10½oz) onion, diced
milk or butter, for mashing (optional)
salt and freshly ground black pepper

Put the potatoes in a pan with enough water to cover: the pot should be big enough that the potatoes only fill it halfway. Add the carrots on top of the potatoes and finish with the onion. Sprinkle 1 teaspoon of salt into the water, cover, and bring to the boil. Cook for about 20 minutes, or until the vegetables are soft.

Drain the pan, saving some of the water. Mash the potatoes, carrots and onions so that the carrots and onions are well distributed throughout the mashed potatoes. Adjust the seasoning to taste. If the *stamppot* is too dry, add 1 tablespoon of the drained cooking liquid at a time. If you prefer, you can also add a little milk or butter to make it richer.

Transfer the *stamppot* to a large platter or bowl.

Serves 4

GF V Veg Use non-dairy milk and butter.

sauerkraut stamppot

see variations page 122

In the wintertime you will see large vats of fresh sauerkraut at Dutch greengrocers, which they scoop out of the vats into transparent plastic bags. Many people sneak a bite or two on their way home: the sweet tanginess of fresh sauerkraut is hard to resist.

1kg (2lb 3oz) floury potatoes (such as Desiree, King Edward, Maris Piper), quartered
500g (1lb 2oz) sauerkraut
1 x 250g (9oz) smoked rope sausage
milk or butter, for mashing (optional)
salt and freshly ground black pepper

Put the potatoes in a pan with enough water to cover: the pan should be big enough that the potatoes only fill it halfway. Sprinkle 1 teaspoon of salt into the water, cover, and bring to the boil for 10 minutes. In the meantime, drain the sauerkraut in a colander, but don't discard the juice. Squeeze any remaining juice out of the sauerkraut and place the sauerkraut on top of the potatoes. Cover, and let it cook for another 10 minutes, adding the sausage for the last 5 minutes of the cooking time.

Remove the sausage from the pan and set aside. Drain the potatoes, saving some of the cooking liquid. Mash the potatoes and sauerkraut so that the sauerkraut is well distributed throughout the potatoes. Adjust the seasoning to taste. If the potatoes and sauerkraut are too dry, add 1 tablespoon of the drained cooking liquid at a time. Or if you prefer a tangier flavour, use the sauerkraut juice. You could also add a little milk or butter to make it richer. Transfer the *stamppot* to a large platter or bowl. Slice the sausage and serve on top.

Serves 4

GF Use a gluten-free sausage.
V Use a vegetarian sausage. **Veg** Use a vegan sausage.

kale stamppot

see variations page 123

This is the classic kale dish that people think of when you ask for *stamppot*. It's not even called *stamppot*; often people will just call it *boerenkool* (kale). A wholesome, hearty meal for cold winter nights. A dollop of mustard is often served on the side.

1kg (2lb 3oz) floury potatoes (such as Desiree, King Edward, Maris Piper), quartered
1kg (2lb 3oz) kale
1 x 250g (9oz) smoked rope sausage
milk or butter, for mashing (optional)
salt and freshly ground black pepper

Put the potatoes in a pan with enough water to cover: the pan should be big enough that the potatoes only fill it halfway. Sprinkle 1 teaspoon of salt into the water, cover, and boil for 10 minutes. In the meantime, remove and discard the stalks from the kale: you can either cut along the stalk with a knife or tear the leaves off the stalk. Wash and rinse the leaves, then roll up several leaves at once and slice the roll once lengthways, and then into short strips. After 10 minutes, add the chopped kale leaves to the pan. Cover, and continue to boil for a further 10 minutes, adding the sausage on top of the kale for the last 5 minutes of cooking.

Remove the sausage from the pan and set aside. Drain the potatoes and kale, saving some of the water. Mash the potatoes and kale so that the kale is well distributed throughout the mashed potatoes. Adjust the seasoning to taste. If the *stamppot* is too dry, add 1 tablespoon of the drained cooking liquid at a time. If you prefer, you can also add a little milk or butter to make it richer. Transfer the *stamppot* to a large platter or bowl. Slice the sausage and serve on top.

Serves 4

GF Use a gluten-free sausage.
V Use a vegetarian sausage. **Veg** Use a vegan sausage.

spinach stamppot

see variations page 124

Fresh spinach is a delicious addition to this *stamppot*: folded in at the last minute, the crispness of the leaves is a nice contrast to the velvety smooth mashed potatoes.

1kg (2lb 3oz) floury potatoes (such as Desiree, King Edward, Maris Piper), quartered
500g (1lb 2oz) spinach leaves
pinch of nutmeg
milk or butter, for mashing (optional)
salt
4 poached eggs, to serve

Put the potatoes in a pan with enough water to cover: the pan should be big enough that the potatoes only fill it halfway. Sprinkle 1 teaspoon of sea salt into the pan, cover, and bring to the boil for 20 minutes, or until the potatoes are soft.

If the stems on the spinach are tough and fibrous, remove them. Wash and drain the spinach leaves and chop roughly.

Drain the potatoes, saving some of the water. Mash the potatoes and fold in the chopped spinach just before serving. Adjust the seasoning with salt to taste and add the pinch of nutmeg. If the *stamppot* is too dry, add 1 tablespoon of the drained cooking liquid at a time. If you prefer, you can also add a little milk or butter to make it richer.

Transfer the *stamppot* to a large platter or bowl and serve immediately, topped with the poached eggs.

Serves 4

GF V Veg Use non-dairy milk and butter and omit the eggs.

brussels sprout stamppot

see variations page 125

The bitterness of the sprouts and the slight sweetness of the potato make for a delicious *stamppot*, even for those who claim not to like Brussels sprouts. For kids, fold in a generous tablespoon of apple sauce (see page 162) to mask some of the bitterness. This *stamppot* pairs well with sausages and onion gravy (see page 132).

1kg (2lb 3oz) floury potatoes (such as Desiree, King Edward, Maris Piper), quartered
500g (1lb 2oz) fresh or frozen Brussels sprouts
1 tbsp coarse grain mustard
milk or butter, for mashing (optional)
salt

Put the potatoes in a pan with enough water to cover: the pan should be big enough that the potatoes only fill it halfway. Sprinkle 1 teaspoon of sea salt into the pan, cover, and bring to the boil for 10 minutes.

If your sprouts are not peeled, remove the outer, tougher leaves, trim the hard stem end and use the knife to carve an X in the stem end. This will help to soften the vegetable. If your sprouts are peeled and fresh, or if they're frozen, there is no need to do this. After 10 minutes, add the sprouts to the pan, cover, and continue to boil for a further 10 minutes.

Drain the potatoes and sprouts, saving some of the water. Mash the potatoes and sprouts and fold in the mustard. Adjust the seasoning to taste. If the *stamppot* is too dry, add 1 tablespoon of the drained cooking liquid at a time. If you prefer, you can also add a little milk or butter to make it richer. Transfer the *stamppot* to a large platter or bowl and serve immediately.

Serves 4

GF Use gluten-free mustard. **V Veg** Use non-dairy milk and butter.

sauerkraut casserole

see variations page 126

Traditionally, Dutch meals consist of potatoes, vegetables and meat. The vegetables are either served by themselves (see pages 142–189) or mashed into the potatoes (see pages 79–91). But every now and then, all three elements find themselves in one casserole.

1 tbsp butter, for greasing
750g (1lb 10oz) potatoes (such as Desiree, King Edward, Maris Piper), boiled
2 tbsp yellow or stoneground mustard
350g (12½oz) sauerkraut
250g (9oz) smoked bacon rashers, cooked
salt and freshly ground black pepper

Preheat the oven to 190°C (375°F). Butter a 20 x 20cm (8 x 8in) ovenproof dish.

Slice the potatoes 5mm (¼in) thick and divide into three equal portions. Line the bottom of the casserole dish with the first portion and brush a little mustard over the slices. Add half of the sauerkraut on top, then 3 rashers of bacon. Add a second layer of potato slices, brush again with the mustard, then top with the remaining sauerkraut and bacon. Finish with a layer of potatoes, brushed with the last of the mustard.

Cover the dish with aluminium foil and bake on the middle shelf of the oven for 30 minutes, removing the foil for the last 10 minutes.

Serves 4

GF Use gluten-free mustard.

beef stew

see variations page 127

Cold winter nights simply beg for a serving of flavourful stewed beef served with mashed potatoes and steamed leeks. Luckily, the recipe is right here!

500g (1lb 2oz) stewing steak, cubed
50g (1¾oz) butter
1 medium onion, sliced into rings
300ml (10½fl oz) hot beef stock
1 sprig of fresh thyme
3 bay leaves
2 tbsp red wine vinegar
2 tsp cornflour mixed with 2 tsp cold water (optional)
salt and freshly black ground pepper

Pat the meat dry and season with a pinch each of salt and pepper. Heat half of the butter in a frying pan or cast-iron casserole. Add the onion rings and sauté for 5 minutes until translucent. Remove the onions from the pan and set aside.

Add the remaining butter to the pan and, when it's hot, brown the meat on all sides. Return the onions to the pan with the stock, thyme, bay leaves and vinegar. Reduce the heat to a simmer, cover, and cook until the meat is tender, 1½–2 hours.

If the gravy is too thin, carefully remove the meat from the pan and heat the remaining juices with half of the cornflour mixture. Stir, adding more if you want a thick sauce. Return the meat to the pan and serve.

Serves 4

GF Use gluten-free stock.

braised beef with cloves

see variations page 128

Braising steak is great for low and slow cooking. The meat becomes tender and provides a great pan gravy, perfect for *hutspot* (see page 83) and steamed cabbage.

500g (1lb 2oz) braising steak, cubed
50g (1¾oz) butter
1 medium onion, sliced into rings
1 tbsp tomato purée
300ml (10½fl oz) hot beef stock
2 cloves
2 bay leaves
1 tbsp red wine vinegar
2 tsp cornflour mixed with 2 tsp cold water (optional)
salt and freshly ground black pepper

Pat the meat dry and season with a pinch each of salt and pepper. Heat half of the butter in a frying pan or cast-iron casserole. Add the onion rings and sauté for 5 minutes until translucent. Stir in the tomato purée and fry for 1 minute, making sure it doesn't burn. Remove the onions from the pan and set aside.

Add the remaining butter to the pan and, when it's hot, brown the meat on all sides. Return the onions to the pan with the stock, cloves, bay leaves and vinegar. Reduce the heat to a simmer, cover, and cook until the meat is tender, about 2 hours.

If the gravy is too thin, carefully remove the meat from the pan and heat the remaining juices with half of the cornflour mixture. Stir, adding more if you want a thicker sauce. Return the meat to the pan and serve.

Serves 4

GF Use gluten-free stock.

hunter's stew

see variations page 129

Nothing speaks to the frugal heart of the Dutch more than being able to use leftovers in another delicious meal. Some will even cook a little extra to ensure a comforting casserole during the week. If you don't have leftover meat, use stewing steak, and increase the cooking time to 90 minutes so that the meat is tender; you may also need to check and adjust the amount of stock. Serve with bread to mop up the juices.

1 large onion, diced
30g (1oz) butter, plus extra for greasing
1 tbsp plain flour
500g (1lb 2oz) cooked roast beef, cut into bite-sized pieces
2 cloves
1 bay leaf
350ml (12fl oz) beef stock
750g (1lb 10oz) potatoes, quartered
1 small red apple
50g (1¾oz) dried breadcrumbs
salt and freshly ground black pepper

Fry the onion in half of the butter until slightly browned, about 5 minutes, then sprinkle over the flour, a pinch of salt and pepper, and add the beef, cloves and bay leaf. Stir in the stock, cover and simmer over a low heat for 30 minutes. In the meantime, boil the potatoes in lightly salted water for 20 minutes. Core and quarter the apple and add to the potatoes for the last 10 minutes of the cooking time. Drain and roughly mash the potatoes and apples, leaving chunks of both.

Preheat the oven to 190°C (375°F). Grease a casserole dish with butter. Place a layer of mashed potatoes in the bottom of the dish. Place the meat and its sauce on top, and finish with another layer of potato. Sprinkle the breadcrumbs on top, fleck with the remaining butter and cook for 30 minutes, or until the top is golden brown.

Serves 4

GF Use gluten-free flour, stock and breadcrumbs.

meatballs

see variations page 130

Dutch meatballs are made with both pork and beef, and their size is somewhere between a golf ball and a tennis ball. Often served with gravy, they can also be eaten hot or cold on a bap or deep-fried with onion slices. Here they are served with rice and peas.

300g (10½oz) minced pork
300g (10½oz) minced beef
1 egg
50g (1¾oz) fresh breadcrumbs
1 tbsp milk or water
1 tsp yellow or stoneground mustard
pinch of nutmeg
1 tsp salt
½ tsp freshly ground black pepper
50g (1¾oz) butter, for frying

Add all the ingredients except the butter to a bowl and use your hands to mix the meat thoroughly for a good 5 minutes, or until everything is well combined. Pinch off a small amount to make a small patty. Fry this in a little butter and taste to see if you want to adjust the seasonings. When you are happy with the seasoning, divide and shapes the mixture into 4 large or 12 small meatballs.

Heat the butter in a pan with a lid, one that the meatballs will fit snugly in. Brown them all over for 2 minutes over a medium-high heat. Once they're browned, add enough water to cover them up to one-third. Reduce the heat, cover, and simmer for 20–30 minutes, or until cooked through. Remove the meatballs from the pan and keep them warm. Bring the liquid up to the boil and reduce for a few minutes, then turn off the heat. Return the meatballs to the pan and serve with the cooking juices.

Serves 4

GF Use gluten-free breadcrumbs and mustard.

roast chicken

see variations page 131

During the 1970s, one of the highlights of my week as a child was going over to Grandma's on Sunday for lunch: *kip*, or roast chicken with homemade chips, asparagus or peas and a large serving of apple sauce (see page 162). Use the chicken seasoning listed here, or your favourite one.

2 tsp flaky sea salt
1 tbsp celery seeds
1½ tsp sweet paprika
1 tsp mustard powder
1 tsp ground ginger
1 tsp onion powder
½ tsp ground coriander
2 bay leaves, crushed
⅛ tsp freshly ground black pepper
⅛ tsp freshly ground white pepper
⅛ tsp ground cardamom
⅛ tsp ground cumin
pinch each of nutmeg and ground cinnamon
1.5kg (3lb 5oz) chicken portions
50g (1¾oz) butter
200ml (7fl oz) water or chicken stock

In a bowl, mix the salt with all of the spices. Rub the chicken pieces with the spice mix and rest for a minimum of 30 minutes or overnight in the fridge.

Heat the butter in a pan large enough to fit the chicken in one layer and fry the chicken pieces until golden, about 10 minutes. Add the water or chicken stock, reduce the heat to low, cover, and braise for 45 minutes, or until the chicken is cooked through.

Serves 4

GF Use gluten-free stock.

bacon-wrapped sausages

see variations page 132

The '*slavink*', short for *slager's vink* (butcher's finch), is not a bird but a delicious sausage wrapped in bacon. They're easy to make and tasty hot or cold.

300g (10½oz) minced pork
300g (10½oz) minced beef
1 tsp salt
½ tsp freshly ground black pepper
⅛ tsp grated nutmeg
1 egg, beaten
125g (4½oz) dried or panko breadcrumbs
16 rashers of streaky bacon
50g (1¾oz) butter

Put the pork, beef and seasoning into a bowl. Stir in the egg, then add the breadcrumbs. Use your hands to knead the mixture for 1–2 minutes until it does not fall apart if you make a small ball in your hand. Divide the mixture into 8 portions. Roll each one into a ball, then, using your fingers, roll them into sausages about 23cm (9in) long. Lay the bacon on a work surface, cover with cling film, and use a rolling pin to roll over it in both directions so the rashers increase in size a little. Lay one sausage lengthways on a rasher and fold both ends over the top. Lay the wrapped sausage widthways on a second rasher and repeat the process, so that the sausage is covered in bacon. Make sure that both ends of the second rasher end up on the same side of the sausage. Repeat with the remaining sausages.

Heat the butter in a frying pan large enough to fit the sausages in one layer. Placing the side that has the ends face down in the pan, carefully press down on the sausages with a spatula or fork for a minute until that side has sealed. Now brown the sausages, carefully rolling them over once or twice, for about 10 minutes. Add 175ml (6fl oz) water to the pan, reduce the heat to low, cover, and simmer for 15 minutes, or until the sausages are cooked through.

Serves 4

GF Use gluten-free breadcrumbs.

pork belly slices

see variations page 133

The Dutch ate pork belly years before it became fashionable! It was never a fancy cut or a gourmet meal, but just like many of our other dishes, a comfort to the soul when done correctly. Some swear by crispy slices of belly, others prefer it soft and tender in a pan gravy – use the recipe below to decide which one you prefer. Serve with *stamppot* or boiled potatoes and vegetables.

1 tsp salt
½ tsp freshly ground black pepper
½ tsp paprika
½ tsp onion powder
500g (1lb 2oz) pork belly slices, about 5mm (¼in) thick
30g (1oz) butter

Mix the salt and seasoning together in a bowl, then season the pork belly slices on both sides.

Heat the butter in a frying pan large enough to fit the slices in one layer, and fry the pork belly slices until brown, about 5 minutes on each side.

For crispy slices, continue to fry for another 2 minutes on each side. For tender pork belly, add 100ml (3½fl oz) water to the pan, cover, reduce the heat and simmer for 5 minutes.

Serves 4

GF

braised pork chops

see variations page 134

Pork chops – *karbonades* – are such a versatile choice: they can be pan-fried, served with a sauce, or braised as they are here. They are delicious served with 'hot lightning' (see page 80) and onion gravy (see page 132).

4 pork chops (about 1kg/2lb 3oz in total)
1 tsp salt
¼ tsp freshly ground black pepper
¼ tsp nutmeg
40g (1½oz) butter, plus extra if needed
4 onions, sliced
2 tbsp plain flour
350ml (12½fl oz) chicken or vegetable stock
1 bay leaf

Pat the meat dry. Mix the salt, pepper and nutmeg and use to season the pork chops.

Heat the butter in a frying pan with a lid and, when it starts to brown, quickly fry the chops on each side for 2 minutes, then reduce the heat and cook for another 5 minutes, turning occasionally, or until cooked through. Remove from the pan and keep warm.

In the same frying pan, slowly fry the onions over a low heat until browned, about 15 minutes. If there is not enough fat, add a little more butter. Sprinkle the flour over the onions and stir carefully to coat, about 2 minutes. Add the stock and keep stirring until the gravy comes together, about 5 minutes. Add the bay leaf, partially cover the pan, and let simmer over a low heat for 5 minutes, stirring every now and then. Serve the sauce with the cooked pork chops.

Serves 4

GF Use gluten-free flour and stock.

stuffed pork tenderloin

see variations page 135

Pork tenderloin is a Sunday favourite in many Dutch households. It is often served with boiled potatoes or chips, apple sauce (see page 162) and a green salad. This recipe is for a delicious *rollade*, a rolled-up stuffed tenderloin.

750g (1lb 10oz) pork tenderloin (in one piece)
1 tsp flaky sea salt
½ tsp freshly ground black pepper
75g (2¾oz) spinach leaves, stems removed
75g (2¾oz) sun-dried tomatoes, chopped
50g (1¾oz) walnuts, chopped
150g (5¼oz) garlic and herb soft cheese
50g (1¾oz) butter

Butterfly the pork tenderloin, or ask your butcher to do this for you. Season the outside lightly with half of the salt and pepper. Toss the spinach leaves, sun-dried tomatoes and chopped walnuts in a bowl with the remaining seasoning.

Spread the cheese over the inside of the tenderloin, then spread the spinach, tomatoes and walnuts over the cheese. Roll up the tenderloin and tie to secure with cooking twine. Preheat the oven to 200°C (400°F).

Heat the butter in a frying pan and brown the meat on all sides, about 10 minutes. Transfer the tenderloin to a baking sheet or ovenproof dish and roast for 10 minutes on one side. Turn the meat, reduce the heat to 190°C (375°F), and roast for another 20 minutes. Remove from the oven, cover, and leave to rest for 5 minutes before slicing.

Serves 4

GF

nasi goreng

see variations page 136

Indonesian food is well represented in the Netherlands and commonly found on the menu. In Indonesia, *nasi goreng* was traditionally made for breakfast with the leftover rice, meat (see page 136) and vegetables from the night before, and so was different every day. In the Netherlands it is considered dinner. For this dish to be successful, it is best to cook the rice the day before and let it cool. Serve with a helping of refreshing sweet and sour cucumber slices on the side.

300g (10½oz) long-grain rice
100ml (3½fl oz) white wine vinegar
2 tsp granulated sugar
1 large cucumber, unpeeled and cut into 5mm (¼in) slices
2 tbsp neutral oil (such as sunflower, rapeseed)
2 small shallots, chopped
2 garlic cloves, finely chopped
1 small red chilli, chopped (optional)
1 tsp shrimp paste (optional)
250g (9oz) mixed vegetables (green beans, cabbage, bean sprouts, carrots, peas), chopped
2 tbsp sweet soy sauce (kecap manis)
4 eggs
oil for frying
1 spring onion, chopped

Wash the rice three or four times, until the water runs practically clear. Boil the rice following the packet instructions, leave to cool, then store in the fridge overnight. Carefully warm the vinegar, 400ml (14fl oz) water and sugar together so that the sugar dissolves. Place the cucumber slices in a bowl, pour over the vinegar and store in the fridge overnight.

The following day, heat the oil in a frying pan and fry the shallots and garlic until fragrant, about 3 minutes. Add the chilli and/or the shrimp paste, if using, and continue to fry for another 3 minutes. Add the vegetables and stir-fry until cooked, 5–6 minutes. Fold in the rice and keep folding it in until the oil, shallots and garlic coat it, then add the sweet soy sauce.

Keep folding until the rice is coated with the soy sauce and is hot, about 5 minutes. Remove from the heat. In a separate pan, fry the eggs. Serve the rice in individual bowls and top each serving with a fried egg, a sprinkling of spring onions, and the cucumber slices on the side.

GF Use gluten-free sweet soy sauce.

pork satay with peanut sauce

see variations page 137

These marinated meat skewers with a peanut sauce make a great accompaniment to *nasi goreng* (see page 110). We also often eat them for lunch with a soft bap, or as a midnight snack. Choose fattier cuts of meat: if it is too lean, it will dry out on the grill.

1kg (2lb 3oz) pork shoulder, cut into 2.5cm (1in) cubes

for the marinade
3 garlic cloves, crushed
2 tbsp brown sugar
1 small onion, grated
125ml (4½fl oz) sweet soy sauce (kecap manis)
1 tsp salt
⅛ tsp white pepper
1 tsp ground coriander
1 tsp ground cumin
juice of ½ lemon

for the peanut sauce
250g (9oz) smooth peanut butter
2 garlic cloves, crushed
1 tsp ground coriander
1 tsp ground cumin
1 tsp ground ginger
pinch of white pepper
2 tbsp brown sugar
1 tsp chilli sauce (optional)
125ml (4½fl oz) coconut milk
2 tbsp lime or lemon juice

to serve
sliced red chillies, sliced spring onions, lime halves

Combine all the marinade ingredients in a bowl. Stir in the pork and set aside overnight in the fridge. The following day, drain the meat, pat dry and thread onto skewers (4 pieces per skewer). If using wooden ones, soak them in cold water for at least 30 minutes before use to prevent them from burning. Cook over hot charcoal or on the grill for 10 minutes, turning once or twice to get a good char on all sides. You can also cook the meat on a hot griddle or pan for 5 to 6 minutes, or until the meat is slightly charred and cooked through. For the sauce, combine the peanut butter, garlic, spices, sugar and chilli sauce, if using, in a pan. Stir in the coconut milk and bring to a simmer over a low heat for 10 minutes. Just before serving, stir in the lime or lemon juice and pour over the cooked skewers.

Serves 4

GF Use gluten-free sweet soy sauce.

macaroni with a meat sauce

see variations page 138

According to a recent survey, most Dutch households eat a pasta dish at least once a week, if not more, and at least one of those is a meal made with elbow macaroni – short, hollow curved tubes.

300g (10½oz) macaroni
2 tbsp olive oil
500g (1lb 2oz) minced beef
1 large onion, chopped
2 garlic cloves, finely chopped
1 x 400g (14oz) tin chopped tomatoes
200g (7oz) tomato passata
1 tsp dried oregano
1 tsp dried basil
¼ tsp dried thyme
1 bay leaf
grated cheese, such as Parmesan, mature Cheddar, or Gouda, to serve
salt

Cook the pasta according to the packet instructions.

Heat the olive oil in a frying pan and brown the minced beef with the onions and garlic for 10 minutes.

Add a pinch of salt, followed by the chopped tomatoes, passata and herbs and simmer for 30 minutes, half covered, stirring every now and then.

Drain the cooked macaroni and add to the meat sauce. Stir to coat, but do not boil. Serve sprinkled with a heaping of grated cheese.

Serves 4

GF Use gluten-free pasta.

fried cod

see variations page 139

Dutch fishmongers always display a dazzling array of fresh and dried fish, fresh seafood, and a variety of prepared salads and hot fried foods. The *lekkerbek* is always hard to resist: a flaky piece of cod, deep-fried in batter. We often buy it for lunch or as a snack, but it can also be served with boiled or fried potatoes, or with a *stamppot* for dinner.

4 cod fillets (about 150g/5¼oz each), skinless and boneless
250g (9oz) plain flour
330ml (11½fl oz) beer (preferably light lager)
1 egg
½ tsp flaky sea salt
¼ tsp dried dill
pinch of ground white pepper
oil, for deep-frying

Pat the fish dry. Mix the flour with the rest of the ingredients in a bowl to form a thick batter.

Heat a deep-fat fryer to 180°C (350°F).

Dip each piece of fish into the batter. Hold it above the bowl until it has stopped dripping (tapping it on the sides of the bowl will help), then carefully place it in the hot oil. Fry for 4 minutes on each side, or until golden brown. Drain on kitchen towel and serve hot.

Serves 4

poached cod

see variations page 140

Cod loin is a good choice for poaching, but you can also use salmon, if preferred. The key to successful poaching is to ensure that the liquid never boils; a low simmer is sufficient. You can poach in fish stock, milk or water. Serve with boiled potatoes.

2 tsp flaky sea salt
4 cod loins (about 150g/5¼oz each)
750ml (26fl oz) fish stock
125ml (4½fl oz) dry white wine
15g (½oz) fresh parsley, stems and leaves separated
10g (⅓oz) fresh dill
1 tbsp capers
200g (7oz) mayonnaise
1 bay leaf
5 black peppercorns

Sprinkle the salt over both sides of the cod loins about 2 hours before cooking. Put them on a plate lined with kitchen towel to soak up some of the liquid, then cover and store in the fridge.

Bring the stock and white wine to the boil, then reduce the heat to a simmer. Add the parsley stems, bay leaf and peppercorns, then carefully drop the fish into the liquid and simmer for 10 minutes.

In the meantime, chop the dill, parsley leaves and the capers and mix them into the mayonnaise. Set aside.

Lift the fish out of the water. Stir 2 tablespoons of the poaching liquid into the mayonnaise and herb sauce.

Serves 4

GF Use gluten-free stock.

mussels

see variations page 141

As soon as the letter R shows up in the month (from September onwards), Dutch restaurants put mussels on their menu. The province of Zeeland is famous for its mussels, traditionally served in a large pot at the table, with dipping sauces and crusty breads.

4kg (8lb 13oz) fresh mussels, in the shell
15g (½oz) butter
1 medium onion, sliced into rings
1 large carrot, diced
2 celery sticks, cut into half rings
2 bay leaves
30g (1oz) fresh parsley, leaves and stems separated
350ml (12fl oz) dry white wine

Rinse the mussels under cold running water and remove any that have a broken shell. Melt the butter in a large pan and sauté the vegetables for 5 minutes, or until they're translucent and fragrant. Add the bay leaves and parsley stems. Put the mussels on top of the vegetables, add the white wine and cover the pot. Bring to the boil and cook for 5 minutes.

Hold down the lid and give the pan three good shakes so that the mussels at the top end up at the bottom. Return to the heat and cook for another 7 minutes, then remove from the heat and take off the lid (be careful of the steam). Scoop the mussels and vegetables out into a serving bowl with a slotted spoon, discarding any mussels that have not opened. Pass the cooking liquid through a tight-mesh sieve to catch any particles or small pieces of shell. Bring the cooking liquid back to the boil, then pour over the mussels and sprinkle with the chopped parsley leaves.

Serves 4 GF

variations

curly endive stamppot

see base recipe page 79

curly endive & smoked cheese stamppot
Omit the sausage and fold in 100g (3½oz) cubed mature smoked Gouda or Cheddar cheese just before serving. **GF V Veg**

curly endive & toasted spiced cashew stamppot
Omit the sausage. Toss 250g (9oz) cashews with 1 tbsp rapeseed oil, a pinch of sea salt, 1 heaped tsp smoked sweet paprika, a pinch of dried oregano and a pinch of chilli flakes. Heat a cast-iron pan over a medium heat and roast the nuts until fragrant, about 5 minutes. Fold half of the nuts into the *stamppot* and sprinkle the rest on top. **GF V Veg**

curly endive stamppot with bacon & buttermilk sauce
Omit the sausage. Fry 150g (5¼oz) smoked bacon lardons in a frying pan until crispy, about 5 minutes. Set aside. Stir ½ tbsp plain flour into the bacon fat to form a paste, then stir in 250ml (8¾fl oz) buttermilk. Continue to stir over a medium-low heat for 2 minutes until thickened. Fold the bacon into the *stamppot* and serve the buttermilk sauce on the side. **GF**

curried curly endive stamppot
Chop 1 medium onion and toss with 1 tbsp curry powder. Fry the onions in 2 tbsp butter for 5–6 minutes until soft and golden. Fold the onions and curly endive into the mashed potatoes. Slice the sausage and serve on top. **GF**

GF Use a gluten-free sausage and flour. Veg Use dairy-free cheese, milk and butter.

variations

apple & potato stamppot

see base recipe page 80

pear & potato stamppot
Use 500g (1lb 2oz) crisp pears instead of the apples. Peel, core and cut them into large chunks, then cook as directed. **GF V Veg**

onion, apple & potato stamppot
Dice 2 large onions and toss them in a bowl with 1 tsp paprika, a pinch of salt, a pinch each of dried oregano and sage. Heat 2 tbsp butter or oil in a frying pan and sauté the onions until they release their fragrance and are slightly browned, 5–6 minutes. Either fold them in to the finished *stamppot* or use as a topping. **GF V Veg**

curried apple & potato stamppot
Sprinkle 2 tsp of your favourite curry powder over the potato and apple mix before mashing. **GF V Veg**

apple sauce & potato stamppot
Instead of adding the apples to the dish before cooking, use apple sauce (see page 162): warm 300g (10½oz) chunky apple sauce in a small pan on the side, and add it to the drained potatoes just before mashing. **GF V Veg**

Veg Use non-dairy milk and butter.

variations

carrot & onion hutspot

see base recipe page 83

parsnip & sweet potato stamppot
Use 400g (14oz) sweet potatoes and 600g (1lb 5oz) parsnips instead of the potatoes. Cook as directed. **GF V Veg**

carrot & onion stamppot with black pudding & apples
Fry 250g (9oz) slices of black pudding (gluten-free if required) and 1 peeled, cored and sliced sweet apple (such as Gala) in 2 tbsp butter until the black pudding has a crispy crust on both sides and the apples are softened, about 10 minutes. Serve on the side with the *hutspot*. **GF**

celeriac, carrot & onion stamppot
Use 800g (1lb 12oz) celeriac instead of the potatoes. Cook as directed. **GF V Veg**

cauliflower & carrot stamppot with caramelised onions
Use 1kg (2lb 3oz) cauliflower instead of the potatoes. Slice the onion rather than dicing, and slowly caramelise the slices in 2 tbsp butter and a pinch of salt for about 10 minutes. Cook the main dish as directed, but reduce the cooking time to 15 minutes. Drain well and let sit, uncovered, to release the steam and slightly dry out the cauliflower before mashing. Top with the caramelised onions. **GF V Veg**

Veg Use non-dairy milk and butter.

variations

sauerkraut stamppot

see base recipe page 84

minced beef & pineapple sauerkraut stamppot
Omit the sausage. Cook 500g (1lb 2oz) minced beef in 2 tbsp butter for 10 minutes, until browned. Season with 1 tsp paprika, ½ tsp onion powder, ½ beef stock cube, 2 squeezes of tomato ketchup, salt and pepper. Stir in 125ml (4½fl oz) water to make a sauce. Drain 1 x 200g (7oz) tin of pineapple chunks and fold into the *stamppot*. Add the beef to a casserole dish and layer the *stamppot* on top. Cover with 75g (2¾oz) dried breadcrumbs, fleck with 30g (1oz) butter and cook at 190°C (375°F) for 20 minutes or until golden. **GF**

bacon & apple sauerkraut stamppot
Omit the sausage. Fry 150g (5¼oz) bacon lardons for 10 minutes, until crisp. Peel and cube 2 sweet apples (such as Gala), and fry in the bacon fat until soft, about 5 minutes, adding 1 tbsp butter if required. Fold into the *stamppot* before serving. **GF**

chorizo sauerkraut stamppot
Omit the sausage. Fry 200g (7oz) diced chorizo for 10 minutes, or until crispy, adding 1 tbsp butter if required. Fold into the *stamppot* and drizzle with the oil from the pan. **GF**

apple & dried cranberry sauerkraut stamppot
Grate 1 sweet apple (such as Gala). Soak a handful of dried cranberries in 125ml (4½fl oz) apple juice for 20 minutes. Drain. Fold into the *stamppot* before serving. **GF**

GF Use a gluten-free sausage, chorizo and breadcrumbs.

variations

kale stamppot

see base recipe page 87

kale, bacon & caramelised onion stamppot
Omit the sausage. Fry 150g (5¼oz) chopped bacon until crispy, adding 1 tbsp butter to the pan if required. Slice 1 onion and caramelise in the fat until golden brown and soft. Fold the bacon through the *stamppot* and serve the onions with a bit of the pan gravy on top. **GF**

kale, sweet potato & red chilli stamppot
Omit the sausage. Use sweet potatoes instead of regular potatoes. Halve, deseed and finely chop 1 large red chilli and fry it in 1 tbsp oil with 2 crushed garlic cloves until fragrant, about 5 minutes. Fold into the finished dish. Sprinkle the frying oil on top. (For a vegan version use dairy-free milk, butter and cheese.) **GF V Veg**

kale & cheese stamppot
Omit the sausage. Fold 100g (3½oz) cubed mature Gouda or Cheddar into the *stamppot* just before serving. (Use dairy-free milk, butter and cheese if required.) **GF V Veg**

kale cakes
Fold 100g (3½oz) plain flour (gluten-free if required) and 1 large egg into the *stamppot* and make into patties weighing about 125g (4½oz) each. Melt 30g (1oz) butter in a non-stick frying pan and fry the patties until golden, 5–6 minutes per side. Slice the sausage and serve on the side.

GF Use a gluten-free sausage.

variations

spinach stamppot

see base recipe page 88

fish goujon & spinach stamppot
Cook 280g (10oz) fish fingers (gluten-free if required) according to the packet instructions. Serve on the side. **GF**

hardboiled egg & spinach stamppot
Boil 4 eggs for 8 minutes. Peel, slice in half lengthways, and serve on the side. Serve with mustard & cream sauce (see page 184) on the side. **GF V**

rocket stamppot
Use rocket leaves instead of the spinach. Cook as directed. **GF V Veg**

salmon, herby cream cheese & spinach stamppot
Mash the potatoes with 75g (2¾oz) garlic and herb soft cheese, fold in the spinach and add 150g (5¼oz) sliced smoked salmon. **GF**

spinach stamppot with grilled halloumi & zaatar
Slice 150g (5¼oz) halloumi cheese in 1.25cm- (½-in) thick slices. Brush lightly with 2 tbsp olive oil. Cook the halloumi in a non-stick frying or grill pan for 3 minutes on each side, or until golden brown. Brush again with 1 tbsp olive oil and sprinkle with 1 tbsp zaatar spices. Serve on the side, or cut into bitesize chunks and mix into the *stamppot* right before serving.

Veg Use non-dairy milk and butter and omit the eggs.

brussels sprout stamppot

see base recipe page 91

bacon & brussels sprout stamppot
Fry 150g (5¼oz) chopped bacon, pancetta or lardons for 10 minutes, or until crispy, adding 1 tbsp butter to the pan if they don't render enough fat. Fold the bacon through the *stamppot* and drizzle a little of the oil over the top. **GF**

sweet potato, sun-dried tomato & brussels sprout stamppot
Use sweet potatoes instead of regular potatoes. Fold in a handful of chopped sun-dried tomatoes marinated in herbs and garlic. **GF V Veg**

caraway cheese & brussels sprout stamppot
Add 150g (5¼oz) cubed Leyden cheese just before serving, or if you can't find Leyden cheese use 1 tsp caraway seeds and 150g (5¼oz) mature Cheddar (non-dairy if required), cut into cubes. **GF V Veg**

sweet potato, brussels sprout & walnut stamppot
Use sweet potatoes instead of regular potatoes. Toast 150g (5¼oz) halved walnuts in a dry frying pan for about 5 minutes, or until they release their fragrance and the colour deepens. Toss with a pinch of dried thyme, a pinch of salt and a pinch of chilli flakes (optional). Mash the sweet potatoes with the sprouts. Fold the nuts into the *stamppot*. **GF V Veg**

GF Use gluten-free mustard. Veg Use non-dairy milk and butter.

variations

sauerkraut casserole

see base recipe page 92

sauerkraut gratin with smoked sausage
Replace the bacon with 1 sliced 250g (9oz) smoked rope sausage. Top with 50g (1¾oz) fresh breadcrumbs and dot with flecks of butter. Bake as directed but do not cover with foil. **GF**

curried sauerkraut gratin with minced beef & pineapple
Omit the bacon. Drain 1 x 200g (7oz) tin of pineapple rings. Brown 500g (1lb 2oz) minced beef in 2 tbsp butter. Add 1 tsp salt, 1 tbsp curry powder, 1 sliced and deseeded red chilli and 100ml (3½fl oz) water and simmer until thick. Place in the dish, top with half the potatoes, the pineapple, sauerkraut and remaining potatoes. Top and bake as above. **GF**

sauerkraut gratin with black pudding & apples
Omit the bacon. Fry 4 slices of black pudding in 2 tbsp butter until crisp. Remove from the pan. Fry 1 cored and sliced sweet apple (such as Gala) until soft. Layer half the potato, the black pudding, apple, sauerkraut and remaining potatoes in a dish. Top and bake as above. **GF**

sauerkraut gratin with minced beef & cranberry sauce
Omit the bacon. Cook 500g (1lb 2oz) minced beef as for the curry variation but season with 1 tsp sweet paprika, 1 tsp salt, a pinch of dried oregano, 1 crushed garlic clove, 1 chopped shallot and 2 tbsp tomato ketchup. Place in the dish, top with 200g (7oz) cranberry sauce, half the potatoes, the sauerkraut and remaining potatoes. Top and bake as above. **GF**

GF Use gluten-free mustard, breadcrumbs and sausage or black pudding.

variations

beef stew

see base recipe page 95

goulash

Omit the thyme, bay leaves and vinegar. Cook the onion in half the butter, then stir in 2 tbsp tomato purée, 2 crushed garlic cloves, 2 tsp paprika, 2 sliced red peppers and 1 tsp caraway seeds. Cook until you can smell the caraway. Add the remaining butter and brown the beef, then stir in the stock. Cover and cook as directed. **GF**

beef in ale (*zuurvlees*, a Limburg speciality)

Omit the onion, stock and thyme. Marinate the beef in 150ml (5¼fl oz) red wine vinegar, 330ml (11½fl oz) dark ale, 3 bay leaves and 3 cloves for 2 hours. Drain, saving the marinade. Season the meat with salt and pepper. Heat the butter in an ovenproof dish and brown the meat. Add the marinade, 1 tbsp brown sugar or apple sauce (see page 162), and ⅛ tsp each of ground cinnamon, coriander and ginger. Cover and cook as directed. Serve over chips. **GF**

hachee (beef & onion stew)

Use 3 sliced onions and add 2 cloves and 1 tbsp plain flour (gluten-free if required). **GF**

beef in red wine

Fry the onion with 1 sliced carrot, 2 sliced celery sticks, 100g (3½oz) quartered mushrooms and 2 crushed garlic cloves until the onions are translucent. Add 200ml (7fl oz) red wine, the beef stock and 2 tbsp dark balsamic vinegar with the herbs. Cover and cook as directed. **GF**

GF Use gluten-free stock.

variations

braised beef with cloves

see base recipe page 96

braised beef with mustard & white wine
Use 100ml (3½fl oz) dry white wine instead of the vinegar. Stir 1 heaped tbsp mustard into the hot stock before adding it to the meat. Cook as directed. **GF**

braised beef with tomatoes & balsamic vinegar
Add 2 large chopped tomatoes to the sauce with the stock. Use dark balsamic vinegar instead of red wine vinegar. Cook as directed. **GF**

beef braised in dark ale
Replace half of the stock with dark ale or stout. Cook as directed. **GF**

Indonesian-inspired braised beef
Omit the tomato purée, bay leaves, cloves and vinegar. Finely chop the onion and fry in 2 tbsp butter with 2 crushed garlic cloves, 1 small deseeded and chopped red chilli, a 5cm (2in) piece of fresh root ginger (peeled and grated), 1 tsp cumin and 1 tsp ground coriander until the onions are soft, about 5 minutes. Remove from the pan. Brown the beef on all sides, then return the onions to the pan. Pour in 400ml (14fl oz) coconut milk and a crushed lemongrass stem and simmer for 1 hour, or until the meat is tender Remove the lid from the pot for the last 20 minutes of cooking time so the liquid can evaporate: there should be little gravy left. Remove the lemongrass stem before serving. **GF**

GF Use gluten-free stock.

variations

hunter's stew

see base recipe page 99

leek & carrot hunter's stew with sliced potatoes

Omit the apple. Fry 1 sliced and diced leek and 150g (5¼oz) diced carrots with the meat. Slice the boiled potatoes instead of mashing them, and layer up as directed. **GF**

beer & pearl onion hunter's stew

Replace half of the beef stock with bock beer (or a dark ale or stout), and replace the onion with 10–12 pearl onions. Cook as directed. **GF**

sweet potato hunter's stew

Omit the apple. Use sweet potatoes instead of regular potatoes. Mash or slice the sweet potatoes, and layer up as directed. **GF**

red wine & juniper hunter's stew

Replace half of the beef stock with red wine. Add three juniper berries to the sauce with the stock and simmer. Remove the berries before serving. **GF**

GF Use gluten-free flour.

variations

meatballs

see base recipe page 100

meatballs with onions & red peppers
Sauté 2 deseeded and sliced red peppers (or use a 280g/9¾oz jar of roasted red peppers) with 1 small diced onion in 2 tbsp butter until soft and slightly browned, 5–6 minutes. Chop into small pieces and mix into the meatball mixture. Cook as directed. **GF**

cheese-stuffed meatballs
Stuff each meatball with a 2.5cm (1in) cube of your favourite cheese. Mature cheese will add greater flavour, while softer and younger cheeses will make for a melting centre. Cook as directed. **GF**

meatballs with mushrooms & parsley
Finely chop 15g (½oz) parsley leaves and 100g (3½oz) cooked mushrooms and mix into the meatball mixture. Cook as directed. **GF**

bear claw meatballs
Slice the cooked meatballs into four thick slices each. Thread them onto wooden skewers, alternating with equally thick onion slices, beginning and ending with a slice of meat. Heat a deep-fat fryer to 190°C (375°F) and fry for 4 minutes, or until the onion is golden brown. Serve with chips or a soft white bap (gluten-free if required). **GF**

GF Use gluten-free breadcrumbs and mustard.

variations

roast chicken

see base recipe page 103

roast chicken with bacon, mushrooms & winter vegetables

Slice 100g (3½oz) mushrooms, 4 rashers bacon, 2 carrots and 1 onion. Dice 4 potatoes, 1 swede and 1 parsnip. Brown the chicken. Sauté the vegetables and bacon for 5 minutes then top with the chicken, add 100ml (3½fl oz) water, cover and cook for 45 minutes. **GF**

curried roast chicken with pineapple

Replace spices with 2 tbsp curry powder. Cook chicken, then add 1 sliced red pepper, 100g (3½oz) mangetout and 1 x 200g (7oz) tin of pineapple chunks, drained. Cook until peppers are soft. Stir in 150ml (5¼fl oz) double cream and heat but do not boil. Serve with rice. **GF**

roast chicken with potatoes, green beans & onions

Marinate and brown the chicken as directed. Sauté 500g (1lb 2oz) potato chunks and 2 diced onions until the onions are translucent. Add the chicken and 200ml (7fl oz) chicken stock, cover and cook for 20 minutes. Stir in 250g (9oz) cooked green beans just before serving. **GF**

shawarma

Omit the spice mix and butter. Marinate 4 sliced chicken breast fillets in 1 tsp each of ground coriander, cumin and paprika, ½ tsp each of onion powder, salt and black pepper, and a pinch of cinnamon. Fry in 2 tbsp olive oil until brown. Stuff 8 pittas (gluten-free if required) with the chicken, iceberg lettuce and cucumber. Drizzle with tzatziki or garlic sauce. **GF**

GF Use gluten-free stock.

variations

bacon-wrapped sausages

see base recipe page 104

bacon-wrapped sausages with ham & cheese

Mix 125g (4½oz) diced cooked ham into the minced meat mixture. Divide the meat into four portions and make larger sausages. Use 125g (4½oz) cubed mild Gouda or Cheddar to stuff inside the meat rolls (a couple of cubes in each) before wrapping them in bacon. **GF**

bacon-wrapped sausages with onion gravy

Omit the nutmeg and use ¼ tsp dried sage instead. Fry the sausages until brown, then remove from the pan. Fry 1 sliced onion in the fat until translucent, about 3 minutes. Add 150ml (5¼fl oz) dark ale and 150ml (5¼fl oz) beef stock (gluten-free if required) and 1 bay leaf. Return the sausages to the pan, and simmer for 20 minutes. Adjust the salt and pepper to taste. **GF**

bacon-wrapped sausages in tomato sauce

Omit the nutmeg and use ½ tsp Italian dried herbs (or fresh oregano, thyme, basil, parsley) instead. Fry the sausages until brown, then remove from the pan. Add 1 x 400g (14oz) tin of chopped tomatoes to the pan and bring to the boil, then add the sausages back into the pan and simmer for 20 minutes over a low heat. **GF**

gherkin-stuffed bacon-wrapped sausages

Wrap the meat around 1–2 cocktail gherkins before wrapping in bacon. Cook as directed. **GF**

GF Use gluten-free breadcrumbs.

variations

pork belly slices

see base recipe page 105

spicy chilli pork belly slices
Omit the spice mix and butter. Rub the pork belly slices with 4 tbsp Sriracha or hot chilli sauce. Line a baking sheet with baking parchment, place the pork slices on top and roast at 190°C (375°F) for 20 minutes, turning after 10 minutes, until crispy. **GF**

cajun spiced pork belly slices
Omit the spice mix. Rub the pork belly slices with 2 tbsp Cajun seasoning. Heat the butter in a frying pan and brown the pork in the pan for 20 minutes over a low heat, turning the slices after 10 minutes. **GF**

mustard-rubbed pork belly slices
Omit the spice mix. Rub the pork belly slices with 4 tbsp Dijon mustard. Cook them in the butter (see cajun variation) or in the oven (see spicy chilli variation). **GF**

breaded pork belly slices
Season the pork belly slices as described in the base recipe, adding a pinch of nutmeg. Line up three plates for breading: one with 50g (1¾oz) plain flour, (gluten-free if required) one with 2 beaten eggs, and one with 50g (1¾oz) dried or panko breadcrumbs (gluten-free if required). Dredge the pork slices through the flour, tapping to remove any surplus, then through the egg, and finally through the breadcrumbs. Fry the slices in the butter until golden brown on both sides, about 15 minutes. **GF**

variations

braised pork chops

see base recipe page 106

italian-style pork chops

Omit the nutmeg, onions, flour and stock. Season the chops with salt, pepper and ⅛ tsp dried Italian herbs. Brown for 3 minutes on each side, reduce the heat and add 1 x 400g (14oz) tin of chopped tomatoes and 1 bay leaf. Cover and simmer for 20 minutes. **GF**

beer-braised pork chops

Omit the nutmeg, flour and stock. Season the chops with salt and pepper and fry as directed. Slice 1 carrot, 1 onion and 2 celery sticks, and sauté for 3 minutes. Add the meat and 330ml (11½fl oz) dark ale. Cover and simmer for 20 minutes. Remove meat and reduce sauce. **GF**

pork chops in a mustard cream sauce

Omit the onions. Season and fry the chops as directed. Remove from pan. Stir 30g (1oz) plain flour into the fat, then 100ml (3½fl oz) water and 100ml (3½fl oz) double cream, then 2 tbsp Dijon mustard. Stir for 1 minute, then simmer for 10 minutes. **GF**

pork chops with pears, thyme & balsamic vinegar

Omit the nutmeg, onions and flour. Season the chops with 3 tsp chopped fresh thyme, salt and pepper. Peel, core and quarter 1 firm pear. Cook the chops as directed, adding the pears for the final 10 minutes. Stir in 4 tbsp white balsamic vinegar, bring to a boil, then reduce the heat. Remove the meat and pears, add 3 tbsp water, boil, then pour over the chops. **GF**

GF Use gluten-free flour and stock.

variations

stuffed pork tenderloin

see base recipe page 109

bacon-wrapped pork tenderloin with a mushroom stuffing
Omit stuffing. Sauté 1 finely chopped onion with 150g (5¼oz) mushrooms and a pinch dried rosemary and thyme in 30g (1oz) butter, until onions are transparent. Prepare pork and wrap with 16 rashers of streaky bacon; secure with cooking twine. Brown and cook as directed. **GF**

pork tenderloin with mushroom sauce
Omit stuffing. Season meat, brown and roast at 220°C (425°F) for 10 minutes. Lower heat to 200°C (400°F), cook for 15 minutes. Fry 1 chopped onion until translucent, add 200g (7oz) sliced mushrooms and cook until starting to brown. Stir in 30g (1oz) plain flour (gluten-free if required), add 250ml (8¾fl oz) stock (gluten-free if required), 1 bay leaf, 75ml (2¾fl oz) double cream; simmer for 15 minutes. **GF**

pork tenderloin with apples
Omit stuffing. Season the meat, brown in butter, reduce the heat and cook for 15 minutes. Remove from the pan. Fry 2 cored and quartered red apples until golden then remove. Deglaze the pan with 100ml (3½fl oz) apple juice. **GF**

pork tenderloin with peppercorn sauce
Prepare and cook the meat as for the tenderloin with apples. Sauté 1 chopped shallot until translucent. Reduce heat and add 350ml (12fl oz) beef stock and 45ml (1½fl oz) brandy. Reduce by three-quarters. Add 1 tbsp brined green peppercorns; simmer for 5 minutes. **GF**

variations

nasi goreng

see base recipe page 110

nasi goreng with ham & leeks
Add 250g (9oz) cubed cooked ham and 1 thinly sliced leek when frying the shallots and garlic. **GF**

nasi goreng with prawns
After frying the vegetables, add the shallots and garlic and then 200g (7oz) peeled raw prawns. Stir-fry for a couple of minutes, then add the rice. **GF**

stir-fried noodles with chicken
Use 300g (10½oz) cooked egg noodles (gluten-free if required) instead of the rice. Add 250g (9oz) diced chicken breast when frying the shallots and garlic. Cook for about 10 minutes, or until the chicken is done. The fried egg is optional. **GF**

nasi goreng with cauliflower rice
Use 500g (1lb 2oz) cauliflower rice, cooked according to the package instructions, instead of the long-grain rice. Cook as directed. **GF**

GF Use gluten-free sweet soy sauce.

variations

pork satay with peanut sauce

see base recipe page 113

chicken satay with peanut sauce
Use 1kg (2lb 3oz) chicken (preferably leg and thigh meat) instead of the pork. Cook as directed. **GF**

lamb satay with peanut sauce
Use 1kg (2lb 3oz) boneless lamb shoulder, sirloin or leg instead of the pork. Cook as directed. **GF**

fish or prawn satay with peanut sauce
Instead of the pork, marinate 1kg (2lb 3oz) firm white fish (such as cod), cut into cubes, or large peeled raw prawns for 2–3 hours (not overnight). Reduce the grilling time to 5 minutes. **GF**

tofu satay with peanut sauce
Instead of the pork, marinate 750g (1lb 10oz) extra-firm tofu, cut into cubes, for 2–3 hours (not overnight). Grill the tofu for 4–5 minutes, turning every minute. **GF V Veg**

GF Use gluten-free sweet soy sauce.

variations

macaroni with a meat sauce

see base recipe page 114

ham & cheese macaroni gratin

Omit the beef, oil, tomatoes, passata and onion. Make a bechamel sauce (see page 161) using 30g (1oz) butter, 30g (1oz) plain flour and 300ml (10½fl oz) milk. Add the garlic, herbs and a pinch of nutmeg; simmer for 10 minutes. Add 150g (5¼oz) cubed ham, 250g (9oz) grated cheese and the macaroni. Place in a dish and top with 60g (2oz) dried breadcrumbs (gluten-free if required), fleck with 20g (¾oz) butter and bake at 190°C (375°F) for 30 minutes. **GF**

mini meatball & cherry tomato macaroni

Omit the tomatoes. Season the beef with 1 tsp salt and ¼ tsp pepper, roll into 2.5cm (1in) meatballs and brown in the oil. Add the onions and garlic and cook until translucent. Stir in the passata and simmer for 10 minutes, then add 200g (7oz) halved cherry tomatoes and cook for 3 minutes. Add ½ tsp each of dried oregano and basil and the macaroni. **GF**

mushroom & black olive macaroni

Omit the beef. Fry onion, garlic and 350g (12½oz) sliced mushrooms in 2 tbsp olive oil. Add tomatoes, passata, herbs and 150g (5¼oz) black olives. Simmer for 10 minutes. **GF V Veg**

smoked salmon & broccoli macaroni

Prepare the ham & cheese macaroni gratin, replacing ham with 250g (9oz) smoked salmon. Stir in 150g (5¼oz) broccoli florets and simmer until cooked before adding the cheese. **GF**

GF Use gluten-free pasta.

variations

fried cod

see base recipe page 116

fried cod bites (*kibbeling*)

Cut the cod into bite-sized pieces, about 2.5–4cm (1–1½in), then batter and fry until golden on all sides, about 3 minutes. Serve with tartare sauce.

fried cod with creamy leeks

Cut 2 large leeks into 5cm (2in) pieces, cut them in half lengthwise and rinse under running water. In a pan, melt 30g (1oz) butter. Add the leeks, cut side down, with 250ml (8¾fl oz) water or vegetable stock. Cover and simmer for 20 minutes, or until softened. Stir in 125ml (4½fl oz) double cream, bring to the boil, then simmer, uncovered, for 10 minutes, or until the sauce has thickened. Season with salt, white pepper and grated nutmeg.

cod burger

Cut an even 10cm (4in) piece from each fish (use the rest for fried cod bites, see above). Coat in the batter and fry for 4 minutes on each side, or until golden brown. Serve on a toasted bun with lettuce, tomato and tartare sauce.

mustard-coated fried cod

Pat the fish dry. Rub each fillet with 1 tbsp coarse grain mustard (gluten-free if required), return to the fridge for 30 minutes. Wipe off any excess mustard with a paper towel and dust the fillets lightly with 2 tbsp plain flour. Tap to remove any loose flour. Make the batter and fry the fish as directed.

variations

poached cod

see base recipe page 117

cod, tomato, olive & red pepper stew
Omit the mayonnaise, dill and capers. Fry 1 chopped onion and 3 crushed garlic cloves in 2 tbsp olive oil until golden. Add 1 x 400g (14oz) tin of chopped tomatoes and a 280g (9¾oz) jar of roasted red peppers, chopped, 1 bay leaf, 1 tsp salt and ¼ tsp black pepper. Stir in 50g (1¾oz) chopped black olives. Simmer for 20 minutes. Spoon over the fish and sprinkle with parsley. **GF**

cod in white wine sauce
Omit the mayonnaise and parsley. Melt 30g (1oz) butter and fry 2 finely chopped shallots, 1 diced carrot and 2 diced celery sticks until soft. Strain the poaching liquid into the pan. Cook until reduced by half. Remove the vegetables. Add 250ml (8¾fl oz) dry white wine and reduce by half. Stir in 125ml (4½fl oz) double cream and the dill. Pour over the fish. **GF**

cod in parsley sauce
Omit the mayonnaise, dill and capers. Make the white wine sauce (see above). Stir in a small handful of chopped parsley leaves right before serving. **GF**

cod in mustard sauce
Omit the mayonnaise, dill and capers. Melt 30g (1oz) butter and stir in 30g (1oz) plain flour (gluten-free if required). Add 450ml (16fl oz) of the strained poaching liquid and 2 tbsp coarse grain mustard (gluten-free if required), and stir until it coats the back of a spoon. **GF**

GF Use gluten-free stock.

variations

mussels

see base recipe page 118

deep-fried breaded mussels

Remove the cooked mussels from their shells and dry. Prepare three plates for breading: one with 4 tbsp plain flour (gluten-free if required), one with 2 beaten eggs, and one with 30g (1oz) dried or panko breadcrumbs (gluten-free if required). Roll each mussel in flour, egg and breadcrumbs. Fry in hot oil (190°C/375°F) for 2–3 minutes until golden brown. Drain on kitchen towel and serve hot with tartare sauce. **GF**

mussels gratin

Remove the empty shell from the cooked mussels and discard. Place the mussels, shell-side down, in an ovenproof dish. Add 1 tbsp of the cooked vegetables to each mussel. Sprinkle 75g (2¾oz) panko breadcrumbs (gluten-free if required) over them and dot with butter. Bake at 190°C (375°F) for 13 minutes, then grill for 2 minutes, or until golden brown. **GF**

mussels in curry sauce

Melt 15g (½oz) butter and stir in 15g (½oz) plain flour (gluten-free if required). Stir in the strained cooking liquid and 2 tbsp curry powder, and cook until it coats the back of a spoon. Stir in the mussels. **GF**

mussels in tomato sauce with garlic & herbs

Add 3 chopped garlic cloves, 1 tsp each of dried oregano and thyme and 1 x 400g (14oz) tin of chopped tomatoes to the base recipe. Simmer for 10 minutes, add the mussels and cook as directed. Serve in the pan, with crusty bread alongside. **GF**

vegetables & sides

Vegetables are a big part of our food culture. When asked what's for dinner, whomever is cooking will usually only name the vegetable, and that is sufficient information. 'What are we having for dinner?' 'Cauliflower'. 'Oh, okay!' That's all we need to know. Another big part of our food traditions is bread: wholemeal, white, rolls, filled with dried fruits or covered with whole grains, usually one or two of the three meals a day involves a choice of bread.

white asparagus

see variations page 172

The province of Limburg is famous for many things, but one of their most precious treasures is 'white gold', delicious white asparagus (*witte asperges*) that is grown from April through June each year. Don't discard the peelings, cut ends or the cooking water – they make for a great soup (see page 172)!

1.5kg (3lb 5oz) white asparagus
30g (1oz) butter
handful of fresh parsley leaves, chopped
salt

Trim the ends of the asparagus as they might be woody. Lay each asparagus spear on a cutting board and peel the stem from the cut end towards the tip, thinly and not overlapping.

Using a pan large enough so that they can all lay down flat, place the asparagus in the pan and add enough water to barely cover them. Add 1 teaspoon of salt to the water and bring to the boil, then reduce the heat and simmer for 5–6 minutes or until the asparagus is done (a fork will easily pierce the bottom end). Remove from the water and place them on a platter.

Clarify the butter by slowly melting it in a small pan. As it simmers, the butterfat will separate from the milk solids into a clear yellow liquid and a white sediment. Carefully pour the clear butterfat over the asparagus, then sprinkle over the chopped parsley.

Serves 4

GF V Veg Use non-dairy butter.

endives with ham & cheese

see variations page 173

Witlof, white chicory, is also called *Brussels lof* – chicory from Brussels. It has a slightly bitter taste, which makes it all the more interesting when used in salads and casseroles. Serve with mashed potatoes (see page 182).

4 large endives (about 650g/1lb 7oz in total)
2 tbsp yellow or stoneground mustard
8 slices cooked ham
8 slices Cheddar, plus an extra 150g (5¼oz) grated
butter, for greasing

Slice the endives in half lengthways and remove the hard root end. Blanch in boiling water for 2 minutes, then remove and set aside.

When the endives have cooled, spread a little mustard on each ham slice. Wrap each endive half in a cheese slice and then a ham slice, with the mustard side towards the cheese.

Preheat the oven to 190°C (375°F).

Butter a large ovenproof dish and lay the endives side by side, so they fit snuggly. Sprinkle the grated cheese over the top and bake for 20 minutes, or until the endives are fully cooked: if there is no resistance when you prick the bulkier end of the endives with a fork, they're ready.

Serves 4

GF Use gluten-free mustard.

brussels sprouts with bacon

see variations page 174

Brussels sprouts, or *spruitjes*, are a staple on the Dutch table, whether mashed, boiled or stir-fried. Most people, especially children, will wrinkle their nose when they hear it's sprouts for dinner. Perhaps one of these recipes will make them believers. *Spruitjes* are a valuable source of vitamins B and C and are delicious served with roast meat and potatoes.

1kg (2lb 3oz) Brussels sprouts
1 tsp salt
150g (5¼oz) sliced bacon, pancetta or lardons
1 tbsp butter (optional)

Cut the hard end off the bottom of the sprouts and remove the outer leaves if they are looking rough, then rinse. Add the sprouts to a pan with plenty of water and the salt, and boil over a medium heat for 10–12 minutes. They're ready if you can easily prick the biggest one with a fork. Drain the water and let the sprouts steam dry for 3 minutes.

Meanwhile, fry the bacon, pancetta or lardons in a frying pan, adding 1 tablespoon butter if they don't render enough fat, for about 10 minutes or until crispy. Toss with the cooked sprouts.

Serves 4

GF V See variations. Veg See variations.

honey-glazed carrots

see variations page 175

Carrots first made an appearance in the Netherlands in the seventeenth century. They were brought over from Iran by the VOC, the Dutch East India Company. These first carrots were white, and through cross-pollination the Dutch were able to achieve an orange colour. Whether this was to honour the royal family, the Oranges, we don't know for sure, but the colour certainly caught on!

2 tbsp olive oil
500g (1lb 2oz) baby carrots
1 tbsp butter
1 tbsp honey
handful of chopped fresh parsley leaves
salt and freshly ground black pepper

Heat the oil in a large frying pan over a high heat and add the carrots. Add a pinch of salt and pepper and toss the carrots so that all sides hit the hot pan, for 5–6 minutes until they are roasted. Take the pan off the heat and add the butter and honey.

Reduce the heat to medium-low, return the pan to the hob and cook the carrots for another 5 minutes until they're soft. Toss the parsley leaves in for the last minute, along with a pinch of salt and pepper.

Serves 4

GF V Veg See variations.

leeks in sauce

see variations page 176

Leeks are so versatile: we use them in soups, in casseroles and by themselves as a side dish. They are slightly oniony with a sweet taste and a tender texture when cooked. Seek out leeks with a maximum diameter of 5cm (2in) – anything thicker will be too tough and stringy. Serve with boiled potatoes.

2kg (4lb 6½oz) leeks (about 4 stalks)
30g (1oz) butter
1 tsp cornflour mixed with 1 tsp cold water
salt and freshly ground white pepper

Cut the darkest leaves off the top of the leeks, right where they start to fan out. Slice the leeks in half lengthways, but don't cut through the root end. Holding by the root end, run the leeks under running water, fanning out the layers to remove any dirt. Shake off any remaining water, then cut each stalk into three pieces and remove the root end.

Melt the butter in a large non-stick frying pan with a lid. Place the leeks in the pan cut-side down and simmer in the butter until slightly coloured, about 3 minutes. Sprinkle with a pinch of salt and pepper and pour 100ml (3½fl oz) water into the pan. Bring to the boil, cover, and reduce the heat to low. Braise the leeks until soft and tender, about 20 minutes.

Remove the leeks from the pan, trying to keep them intact. Bring the braising liquid back up to the boil and stir in the cornflour mixture, cooking until it thickens slightly, about 2 minutes. Adjust the salt and pepper to taste, then pour the sauce over the leeks.

Serves 4

GF V Veg Use non-dairy butter.

cauliflower with a creamy sauce

see variations page 177

One of the most popular vegetables in the Netherlands, cauliflower is often served in a white sauce with a pinch of nutmeg and a side of boiled potatoes. Simple but effective.

1–1.5kg (2lb 3oz–3lb 5oz) cauliflower
15g (½oz) butter
15g (½oz) plain flour
milk or vegetable stock, if required
pinch of nutmeg
salt

Use a knife to cut the florets from the stem of the cauliflower. If they are too big, you can cut them in half. Cut the stem into bite-sized pieces. Wash and drain the cauliflower pieces, then add 250ml (8¾fl oz) water to a pot with ½ teaspoon of salt and the cauliflower. Cover and bring to the boil, then reduce the heat to medium-low and steam for 10 minutes, or until the cauliflower is soft when pricked with a fork. Drain, but save the liquid. Let the cauliflower sit uncovered for a few minutes, then keep warm until ready to serve.

Melt the butter in a frying pan and stir in the flour until it forms a thick paste. Measure out the cooking liquid and top up with milk or vegetable stock to 250ml (8¾fl oz) if required. Stir the liquid into the paste a little at a time until it thickens, about 10 minutes. Taste and add more salt if needed. Pour the sauce over the cauliflower, and dress with a pinch of nutmeg to serve.

Serves 4

GF Use gluten-free flour. **V Veg** Use non-dairy butter and vegetable stock.

buttered green beans

see variations page 178

Here *sperziebonen* (green beans) are served in the traditional way, with melted butter and a pinch of nutmeg. But there are so many other ways to put them on the menu, too – see page 178. Try eating them with bacon-wrapped sausages (see page 104) and apple sauce (see page 162).

800g (1lb 12oz) green beans
½ tsp salt
30g (1oz) butter
pinch of nutmeg

Top and tail the beans, cutting any really long ones in half, and give them a quick rinse.

Add 5cm (2in) water to a large pot, add the salt and bring to the boil. Add the beans to the pan, cover, and reduce the heat to a simmer. Cook for 10–12 minutes, or until you can pierce a bean easily with a fork.

Drain the beans and stir through the butter and a pinch of nutmeg.

Serves 4

GF V Veg Use non-dairy butter.

green cabbage with thyme

see variations page 179

Depending on where you live, you may have access to green cabbage, white cabbage or both. Either one works really well for this recipe and its variations (see page 179).

1kg (2lb 3oz) green or white cabbage
30g (1oz) butter
100ml (3½fl oz) water or vegetable stock
1 bay leaf
¼ tsp dried thyme or 4 fresh sprigs of thyme
salt

Remove any tough outer leaves from the cabbage. Cut the cabbage in half through the stem and cut each half into three or four wedges. Remove the hard core at the base. Slice the cabbage into 2.5cm (1in) strips. Wash and drain the cabbage slices.

Melt the butter in a large frying pan and add the cabbage. Sprinkle over a pinch of salt and sauté for 2–3 minutes, then pour in the water or stock, add the bay leaf, bring to the boil, then reduce the heat to a simmer. Cover, and let the cabbage braise for 15 minutes, or until softened.

Sprinkle the thyme over the cabbage just before serving.

Serves 4

GF V Veg Use non-dairy butter.

braised red cabbage

see variations page 180

Red cabbage, with its beautiful dark purple leaves, forms the base of many dishes. Braised with apples, it is often served together with *hachee* or *draadjesvlees* (meat stews) (see pages 99 and 127) and boiled or mashed potatoes (see page 182). In the summertime, red cabbage makes for a tasty coleslaw.

1kg (2lb 3oz) red cabbage
2 sweet, tart apples (such as Jonagold)
1 bay leaf
2 cloves
1 tsp sea salt
1 cinnamon stick (optional)
1 tsp cornflour
1 tbsp granulated sugar (optional)

Remove any tough outer leaves from the cabbage. Cut the cabbage in half through the stem and cut each half into three or four wedges. Remove the hard core at the base. Slice the cabbage thinly. Peel, core and cube the apples.

Simmer the cabbage with 200ml (7fl oz) water, the bay leaf, cloves, salt and cinnamon stick, if using, in a covered pan. After 15 minutes, add the apple pieces and stir once or twice. Continue to simmer for another 10 minutes, or until the cabbage is soft.

Remove the cabbage from the pan, but leave the liquid. Mix the cornflour with 2 teaspoons of water. Bring the cooking liquid up to the boil, stir in the cornflour and stir until the liquid thickens, 2 minutes. Stir in the cabbage. Sweeten with the sugar if necessary.

Serves 4

GF V Veg

spinach with cream

see variations page 181

Spinach is grown year-round in the Netherlands. In the springtime, the leaves are small and tender, and as the season progresses, they become larger and a little bit tougher. We often pair spinach with fish and boiled potatoes.

1kg (2lb 3oz) spinach
20g (3/4oz) butter
125ml (4½fl oz) double cream
pinch of nutmeg
salt

Wash the spinach leaves in a colander and remove any large stalks.

In a large pan, melt the butter and add the cream. Bring to the boil, then reduce the heat and simmer for 2 minutes. Add the spinach, stir a couple of times, and add a pinch of salt and nutmeg. Do not overcook the spinach – cook it for 3 minutes, until the leaves are slightly wilted.

GF V Veg Use non-dairy butter and cream.

duchesse potatoes

see variations page 182

There was a reason why Van Gogh painted *The Potato Eaters* – we love our spuds! *Pommes Duchesse* is best made with floury potatoes such as Maris Piper or King Edward.

1kg (2lb 3oz) potatoes, peeled and quartered
2 egg yolks
45g (1½oz) butter
pinch of nutmeg
salt and freshly ground black pepper

Put the potatoes in a pan with enough water to cover. Sprinkle 1 teaspoon of salt into the water, cover, and bring to the boil. Cook for 20 minutes, or until the potatoes are soft – a knife should slide in without any resistance. Drain the potatoes, then return them to the pan with the lid off to steam dry, about 5 minutes. Toss the pan once or twice so that the top potatoes move to the bottom. Mash the potatoes with the egg yolks and butter until you have a creamy consistency without any lumps. Add salt to taste, with a sprinkling of pepper and a pinch of nutmeg.

Line a baking sheet with baking parchment. Preheat the oven to 190°C (375°F). Fill a piping bag fitted with a star-shaped tip with the mashed potato, and pipe about 12 swirls of mash – 5cm (2in) in diameter and about 4cm (1½in) high – onto the prepared baking sheet. Cook for 20 minutes or until golden brown.

GF V

pickled cucumbers

see variations page 183

Tafelzuur, or mixed pickles, comprise a variety of pickled sweet and sour vegetables that are used as side dishes or condiments. This recipe is for a quick cucumber pickle. Like its variations (see pages 183) they are not suitable for canning or preserving and should be kept refrigerated and consumed within five days.

4 cucumbers
1 litre (1¾ pints) white wine vinegar or distilled vinegar
250g (9oz) granulated sugar
2 bay leaves
10 black peppercorns
1 red chilli, chopped (optional)

Peel the cucumbers, slice them in half lengthways and scoop the seeds out carefully with a spoon. Cut the cucumber into slices, about 5mm (¼in) thick.

In a large pan, heat the vinegar, sugar, bay leaves, peppercorns and chilli if using and stir until the sugar dissolves.

Leave to cool, then pour the cold liquid over the cucumber slices, making sure they are submerged.

Serves 4

GF V Veg

bechamel sauce

see variations page 184

This white sauce, known as a bechamel sauce, makes the perfect partner to our favourite vegetables.

30g (1oz) butter
30g (1oz) plain flour
350ml (12fl oz) milk
1 tsp salt
½ tsp freshly ground black pepper
pinch of nutmeg

Melt the butter in a pan and stir in the flour until a thick paste is formed, about 2 minutes.

Add a quarter of the milk at a time, stirring constantly, until the sauce thickens and bubbles, about 10 minutes.

Season with the salt, pepper, and a pinch of nutmeg.

Serves 4

GF Use gluten-free flour. **V Veg** Use non-dairy butter and milk.

apple sauce

see variations page 185

Appelmoes – apple sauce – is probably the most famous and frequently used sauce at dinner time. To sweeten their food, small children are given apple sauce as a condiment, and the habit tends to remain into adulthood as well, as the sauce is mixed in with *stamppot* or used as a cold, sweet side dish. Apple sauce is best when two or more varieties of apple are used. It can be stored in the fridge for five days.

1kg (2lb 3oz) apples (such as McIntosh, Golden Delicious, Braeburn or Bramley)
125g (4½oz) granulated sugar
2 tbsp lemon juice

Peel and core the apples and cut them into quarters. Add them to a heavy-based pan with just enough water to keep them from sticking; it should come about halfway up the fruit. Bring to the boil, then reduce the heat and simmer for 10–15 minutes, uncovered, until the apples are soft. Remove from the heat.

Purée or mash the apples with a fork or potato masher. Stir in the sugar and lemon juice and return to the heat, stirring until the sugar dissolves and the apples form a thick compote, about 5 minutes. Serve cold.

Serves 4

GF V Veg

cheese & onion bread

see variations page 186

This is a favourite for lunch: best eaten slightly warm with a glass of cold milk.

10g (1/3oz) dried active yeast
250ml (8 3/4fl oz) lukewarm water (no hotter than 46°C/115°F)
350g (12 1/2oz) plain flour
pinch of salt
1 medium onion, sliced
1 tbsp butter
250g (9oz) grated cheese (use a blend of mature cheeses)

Sprinkle the yeast over the warm water and let it sit for 10 minutes, or until bubbly. Combine the flour with the salt in the bowl of a stand mixer and add the yeast and water. Mix to combine, then knead for 10 minutes, or until the dough is smooth. If you are kneading by hand, you will need to do it for 20 minutes. Cover the dough and let it rest in a warm place until doubled in size, about 1 hour.

Sauté the onion slices in the butter until translucent but not browned, about 5 minutes. Set aside. Preheat the oven to 190°C (375°F)

Punch down the dough, then pat and stretch it into a 30 x 15cm (12 x 6in) rectangle. Line a baking sheet with baking parchment and place the dough on top. Distribute the onions over the top, then sprinkle over the cheese. Bake for 20 minutes, or until the cheese has melted and the dough is a golden brown colour. Leave to rest for 5 minutes, then cut it into small squares.

Makes 1 loaf

V Veg Use non-dairy butter and cheese.

wholegrain loaf

see variations page 187

The Dutch have an extensive range of breads: from white to wholemeal, rye to barley, and an array of choices in between. It is not unusual to have more than 30 variations to choose from at the bakery. For breakfast we enjoy wholegrain bread with cheese, cold cuts, tomatoes and cucumbers.

10g (1/3oz) dried active yeast
450ml (16fl oz) lukewarm water (no hotter than 46°C/115°F)
750g (1lb 10oz) wholemeal flour
20g (3/4oz) flaky sea salt
30g (1oz) butter, softened

Sprinkle the yeast over the warm water and let it sit for 10 minutes, or until bubbly and alive. Combine the flour with the salt in the bowl of a stand mixer and add the yeast and water. Mix on low speed for 5 minutes, then add the butter and knead for 10 minutes at medium speed. If you are mixing and kneading by hand, you will need to do it for 20 minutes. Pat the dough into a ball and place it in an oiled bowl. Cover and leave in a warm place to rise for 40 minutes, or until doubled in size.

Grease and flour a 20 x 10cm (8 x 4in) loaf tin. Punch down the dough, then pat and stretch it into a rectangle. Roll it up from the long side like a Swiss roll and place in the prepared tin seam-side down. Cover and leave in a warm place to rise until it is above the rim of the loaf tin, about 1 hour.

Preheat the oven to 190°C (375°F). Brush the top of the bread with a little water and bake for 30 minutes. Take the loaf out of the oven and turn it upside down. Tap it firmly with your index finger or thumb. If the bread sounds hollow, it's done.

Makes 1 loaf

V Veg Use non-dairy spread.

muesli rolls

see variations page 188

These muesli rolls combine the wholesome with the delicious and are definitely worth a try. Many people enjoy eating them spread with butter and jam.

7g (1/4oz) dried active yeast
400ml (14fl oz) lukewarm water (no hotter than 46°C/115°F)
400g (14oz) whole wheat flour
200g (7oz) plain flour
10g (1/3oz) flaky sea salt
150g (5 1/4oz) muesli (with rolled oats, seeds and dried fruits)
20g (3/4oz) butter, melted
50g (1 3/4oz) rolled oats

Sprinkle the yeast over the warm water and let it sit for 10 minutes, or until bubbly and alive.

Combine the flours with the salt in bowl of a stand mixer and add the yeast and water. Mix to combine, then knead for 10 minutes, or until the dough is soft and pliable. If you are kneading by hand, you will need to do it for 20 minutes. Cover the dough and let it rest in a warm place until doubled in size, about 1 hour.

Punch down the dough, then add the muesli and knead it in. Divide the dough into 12 pieces (80g/3oz each) and shape each one into a roll. Brush the rolls with the butter then sprinkle over the oats. Cover and leave in a warm place to rise again, for about 30 minutes or until almost doubled in size.

Preheat the oven to 220°C (425°F) and bake for 20 minutes. Turn one of the rolls upside down and tap it firmly with your index finger or thumb. If the bread sounds hollow, it's done.

Makes 12

V Veg Use non-dairy spread.

white bread

see variations page 189

Dutch breakfasts and lunches often consist of sandwiches. A traditional option is to have one round each of white and wholemeal bread: one with a savoury filling and the other a sweet one, such as jam or chocolate sprinkles. Bread is an essential part of any meal. You can vary the recipe to make sugar bread and cinnamon rolls (see page 189).

10g (1/3oz) dried active yeast
450ml (16fl oz) lukewarm water (no hotter than 46°C/115°F)
750g (1lb 10oz) strong white bread flour
20g (3/4oz) flaky sea salt
30g (1oz) butter, softened
milk, for brushing

Sprinkle the yeast over the warm water and let it sit for 10 minutes, or until bubbly. Combine the flour with the salt in the bowl of a stand mixer and add the yeast and water. Mix on low speed for 5 minutes, then add the butter and knead for 10 minutes at a medium speed. If you are mixing and kneading by hand, you will need to do it for 20 minutes. Pat the dough into a ball and place it in an oiled bowl. Cover and leave in a warm place to rise for 40 minutes, or until doubled in size.

Grease and flour a 20 x 10cm (8 x 4in) loaf tin. Punch down the dough, then pat and stretch it into a rectangle the length of the loaf pan. Roll it up from the long side like a Swiss roll and place in the tin seam-side down. Cover and leave to rise in a warm place until it is above the rim of the tin, about 1 hour. Preheat the oven to 190°C (375°F). Brush the top of the bread with a little milk and bake for 30 minutes, or until a deep golden brown all over. Tap the bottom with a finger; if it sounds hollow it's done.

Makes 1 loaf V

variations

white asparagus

see base recipe page 143

white asparagus with ham & cheese

Cook the asparagus as directed. Lay 4 slices of ham on a plate, place the warm asparagus and 4 halved hardboiled eggs on top. Pour over the melted butter. Dress with the parsley. **GF**

white asparagus soup

Omit the butter. Cook the asparagus as directed. Reserve the spears, cutting the top 5cm (2in) from one-third of them. Simmer the asparagus peelings in the cooking water with 1 vegetable stock cube for 1 hour. Strain the stock and purée with the reserved spears. Add 3 tbsp double cream, the parsley and the reserved tips. Season with black pepper. **GF V Veg**

white asparagus with lemon & dill butter

Soften 60g (2oz) salted butter and mix in ½ tsp chopped fresh dill, 1 tsp lemon zest and 1 tsp lemon juice. Chill until semi-solid, wrap in cling film, roll into a log and chill until required. Cook the asparagus as directed and dot with the butter just before serving. **GF V**

white asparagus with eggs, capers & mustard

Cook the asparagus as directed. Make a bechamel sauce (see page 161) using the butter, 30g (1oz) plain flour and 500ml (17½fl oz) of the cooking water. Add 1 tbsp drained capers and 2 tsp yellow mustard (gluten-free if required); season. Serve with 4 halved hardboiled eggs, boiled potatoes and sprinkled with parsley. **GF V**

GF Use gluten-free stock. Veg Use non-dairy butter and cream.

variations

endives with ham & cheese

see base recipe page 144

endives with prosciutto & mashed potatoes
Omit sliced cheese; replace ham with prosciutto. Line a dish with 750g (1lb 10oz) mashed potatoes. Top with wrapped endives and cheese. Bake for 20 minutes at 190°C (375°F). **GF**

cream of endive soup with potato & ham
Omit cheese and mustard. Soften 1 chopped onion in 1 tbsp butter, repeat with 1 diced potato and sliced endives. Add 1 bay leaf and 750ml (26fl oz) stock (gluten-free if required). Cover, simmer for 15 minutes. Remove bay leaf. Blend, add ham and 8 tbsp double cream. **GF**

endives in a cheese sauce
Omit the ham, mustard and sliced cheese. Make a bechamel sauce (see page 161) using 30g (1oz) plain flour, 30g (1oz) butter and 350ml (12fl oz) milk. Add 1 bay leaf; simmer for 10 minutes. Remove bay leaf. Stir in grated cheese. Arrange blanched endive in a dish, pour over the sauce and bake at 190°C (375°F) for 20 minutes. **GF V**

endive salad
Omit ham and cheese. Combine chopped endives, 1 grated carrot and 1 sliced red pepper. Dress with 1 tsp mustard, 1 tbsp mayonnaise (vegan if required), 2 tbsp plain yoghurt (dairy-free if required) and ½ tbsp white wine vinegar. Top with 25g (¾oz) walnuts and segments from a 200g (7oz) tin mandarins. **GF V Veg**

GF Use gluten-free mustard.

variations

brussels sprouts with bacon

see base recipe page 147

brussels sprouts with nutmeg
Omit the bacon. Toss the cooked sprouts with a little grated nutmeg. **GF V Veg**

warm brussels sprouts, bacon, apple & cranberry salad
Slice the sprouts thinly. Fry the bacon as directed and set aside. Remove the bacon fat from the pan, leaving 1 tbsp behind. Stir-fry the sprout slices for 3 minutes until slightly wilted. Remove the sprouts and stir 2 tbsp cider vinegar or white wine vinegar into the fat. Stir for a few seconds, then remove from the heat. Mix the bacon with the warm sprouts, 75g (2¾oz) dried cranberries and 1 peeled and chopped apple. Toss with the warm vinegar. **GF**

brussels sprouts gratin
Omit the bacon. Put the cooked sprouts in a buttered ovenproof dish. Pour over a bechamel sauce made from 25g (¾oz) butter, 25g (¾oz) plain flour (gluten-free if required), 400ml (14fl oz) milk (non-dairy if required), salt, pepper and nutmeg (see page 161). Top with 50g (1¾oz) breadcrumbs (gluten-free if required), fleck with 25g (¾oz) butter and cook at 190°C (375°F) for 20 minutes, until brown. **GF V Veg**

brussels sprouts with apples, bacon & mustard
Fry the bacon as directed. Peel and core 2 small red apples and cut into thick slices. Cook in 1–2 tbsp of the leftover bacon fat. Toss the bacon and apples with the cooked sprouts and stir in 1 tbsp coarse grain mustard (gluten-free if required). **GF**

Veg Use non-dairy butter.

variations

honey-glazed carrots

see base recipe page 148

balsamic-glazed carrots
Use 2 tbsp white balsamic vinegar instead of the honey. Replace the parsley with ½ tsp dried Italian herbs. **GF V Veg**

honey & caraway glazed carrots
Omit the parsley. Sprinkle 1 tsp caraway seeds in the butter and toss with the carrots. **GF V**

garlic & thyme glazed carrots
Omit the honey and parsley. After roasting the carrots, add 2 crushed garlic cloves with the butter. Sprinkle a little chopped fresh thyme over the carrots 2 minutes before serving. **GF V Veg**

ginger & orange glazed carrots
Omit the parsley. Add 1 tsp freshly grated root ginger and 1 tsp grated orange zest with the butter. Stir and cook with the carrots. **GF V**

Veg Use non-dairy butter.

variations

leeks in sauce

see base recipe page 149

leeks in a cream sauce
Omit the cornflour and stir 100ml (3½fl oz) double cream (dairy-free if required) into the cooking liquid. Simmer until the sauce starts to thicken. Serve over the leeks. **GF V Veg**

leeks with butter, white wine & capers
Omit the cornflour. Stir 125ml (4½fl oz) dry white wine (vegan if required) into the cooking liquid. Bring back up to the boil and simmer for 3–4 minutes, stirring, until the sauce has reduced by a quarter. Take off the heat and stir in 1 tbsp butter and 1 tbsp drained capers. Stir and serve over the cooked leeks. **GF V Veg**

leek gratin
Butter an ovenproof dish. Put the cooked leeks in the dish side by side and pour the sauce over the top. Sprinkle 50g (1¾oz) dried or panko breadcrumbs (gluten-free if required) over the top, dot with 15g (½oz) butter, and cook at 190°C (375°F) for 20 minutes. **GF V Veg**

leeks in a blue cheese sauce
Omit the cornflour. Combine 75g (2¾oz) blue cheese (dairy-free if required) with 250ml (8¾fl oz) double cream (dairy-free if required) and a pinch of pepper and salt. Stir into the braising liquid and simmer until the sauce thickens, about 5 minutes. Return the leeks to the pan and simmer for 2 minutes. **GF V Veg**

Veg Use non-dairy butter.

variations

cauliflower with a creamy sauce

see base recipe page 150

cauliflower with a cheese sauce

Cook the cauliflower as directed. Add enough milk to the leftover cooking liquid to make 250ml (8¾fl oz) and use to make the sauce, as directed. Stir in 100g (3½oz) grated mature Cheddar or Gouda until it has melted, but do not let it boil. **GF V**

cauliflower with a curry sauce

Cook the cauliflower as directed. Add enough coconut milk to the cooking liquid to make 250ml (8¾fl oz) and use to make the sauce. Stir in 2 tsp curry powder. Omit the nutmeg and serve sprinkled with a handful of fresh coriander or toasted flaked almonds. **GF V Veg**

cauliflower with a tomato sauce

Add a vegetable stock cube when steaming the cauliflower. Halve 350g (12½oz) ripe tomatoes and toss with 2 tbsp olive oil, 2 crushed garlic cloves, 1 tsp each of fresh oregano and thyme and a little black pepper. Place on a baking sheet and roast at 230°C (450°F) for 30 minutes, or until the tomatoes are soft and the cauliflower is becoming golden. **GF V Veg**

cauliflower gratin

Cook the cauliflower and sauce as directed. Put the cauliflower in an ovenproof dish, pour over sauce. Sprinkle with 50g (1¾oz) dried or panko breadcrumbs (gluten-free if required), dot with 1 tbsp butter and cook at 190°C (375°F) for 20 minutes, or until brown. **GF V Veg**

GF Use gluten-free flour. Veg Use non-dairy butter and milk.

variations

buttered green beans

see base recipe page 153

green beans with tomatoes & onions
Omit the nutmeg. Dice 2 tomatoes and 1 medium onion, and fry in the butter until soft. Toss with the cooked green beans and season with salt and black pepper. **GF V Veg**

green beans with bacon & onions
Omit the nutmeg. Fry 250g (9oz) chopped bacon until browned. Remove. Fry 1 diced onion in 1–2 tbsp of the fat until translucent. Toss with the bacon and cooked green beans. **GF**

green bean salad
Omit the butter and nutmeg. Cook beans as directed; cut into bite-sized pieces. Halve 100g (3½oz) cherry tomatoes; slice 2 hardboiled eggs and 1 medium carrot. Slice 1 red onion and marinate in 4 tbsp white balsamic vinegar and a pinch of salt for 20 minutes. Drain onion (reserving vinegar) and toss with vegetables. Season with salt and pepper. Combine 2 tbsp of the vinegar, 4 tbsp rapeseed oil and a pinch of dried oregano and serve on the side. **GF V**

indonesian green beans (sambal buncis)
Omit the butter and nutmeg. Cook the beans as for salad above. Fry 3 crushed garlic cloves, 1 chopped onion, 2 diced tomatoes, 1 tbsp red chilli paste, ½ tsp shrimp paste and 1 tsp each ground coriander, cumin and ginger in 2 tbsp light olive oil until tomatoes are soft. Add 350ml (12fl oz) coconut milk and simmer for 10 minutes. Fold in beans. Serve with rice. **GF**

Veg Use non-dairy butter.

variations

green cabbage with thyme

see base recipe page 154

green cabbage in a cream sauce with nutmeg

Cook the cabbage as directed, adding 50ml (1¾fl oz) double cream (dairy-free if required) after the 15 minutes' cooking time. Bring back to the boil, stir and cook until thickened slightly. Omit the thyme and add a pinch of nutmeg to the dish before serving. **GF V Veg**

green cabbage in a cheese sauce

Omit the thyme. Make a bechamel sauce (see page 161) using 15g (½oz) butter, 15g (½oz) plain flour and 250ml (8¾fl oz) braising liquid from the cabbage (if you don't have enough, add a little vegetable stock, milk or water). Add 125g (4½oz) grated cheese (dairy-free if required), stir until melted but do not boil, 1–2 minutes. Pour over the cabbage and sprinkle with paprika. **GF V Veg**

oven-roasted cabbage

Leave the cabbage in wedges. Melt the butter and brush over the cabbage. Sprinkle with a pinch of salt and dried oregano. Roast at 200°C (400°F) for 20 minutes. **GF V Veg**

coleslaw

Thickly slice each cabbage wedge; do not cook. Grate 2 carrots. Mix 150g (5¼oz) mayonnaise (vegan if required) with 2 tbsp cider vinegar, a pinch each of salt and black pepper, 1½ tbsp yellow mustard and 1 tsp celery seeds. Chill for 2 hours before serving. **GF V Veg**

Veg Use non-dairy butter.

variations

braised red cabbage

see base recipe page 155

braised red cabbage with raisins & cinnamon
Cook as directed, adding 50g (1¾oz) sultanas or raisins and a cinnamon stick to the pan with the apples. **GF V Veg**

red cabbage stamppot
Boil and mash 1kg (2lb 3oz) floury potatoes, then stir through the cooked red cabbage to make a stamppot. Remove the bay leaf and cinnamon before adding the cabbage. **GF V Veg**

red cabbage coleslaw
Do not cook the cabbage. Thinly slice each cabbage wedge. Grate 2 carrots and 1 cored red apple. Mix 4 tbsp olive oil with 2 tbsp cider vinegar, a pinch each of salt and black pepper, 1½ tbsp stoneground or yellow mustard and 1 tsp celery seeds. Chill in the fridge for 2 hours before serving. **GF V Veg**

red cabbage with minced beef & potatoes
Fry 500g (1lb 2oz) minced beef in 25g (¾oz) butter with 1 finely chopped onion, 2 finely chopped garlic cloves and a pinch each of salt, pepper and dried thyme, for 15 minutes, or until the meat is browned and the onion and garlic are soft. Place the mixture in a buttered ovenproof dish, add the red cabbage and apples (prepared as directed), and top with 500g (1lb 2oz) mashed potatoes. Make ridges in the top of the mashed potato with a fork and bake at 190°C (375°F) until golden brown and bubbly, about 25 minutes. **GF**

variations

spinach with cream

see base recipe page 156

spinach with scrambled eggs & toast soldiers
Omit the cream and nutmeg. Sauté the spinach in the butter until wilted; season. Scramble 8 eggs with a pinch of salt in 20g (3/4oz) butter. Season with salt and pepper. Toast 4 slices of bread (gluten-free if required), cut off the crusts and cut each slice into 4 pieces. **GF V**

spinach, apple & bacon salad
Omit the butter, cream and nutmeg. Fry 250g (9oz) chopped bacon until crispy, adding 1 tbsp butter to the pan if they don't render enough fat. Set aside and remove all the grease except for 2 tbsp. Deglaze the pan with 30ml (1fl oz) white wine vinegar. Core and cube a red apple. Toss the bacon, spinach leaves and apple with the hot vinegar. Serve immediately. **GF**

quick spinach & feta wrap
Omit the cream and nutmeg. Sauté spinach in butter until barely wilted. Chop and season with salt and pepper. Add a handful of chopped spinach to one side of 4 tortilla wraps (gluten-free if required) and top each with 35g (1 1/4oz) feta cheese (dairy-free if required). Season. Fold over wrap and fry in 1 tbsp light olive oil until golden on both sides. **GF V Veg**

spinach with sultanas
Omit the cream. Add 50g (1 3/4oz) washed and rinsed sultanas to the butter for 2 minutes before adding the spinach when cooking. Sauté until the spinach is slightly wilted. **GF V Veg**

Veg Use non-dairy butter and cream.

variations

duchesse potatoes

see base recipe page 159

mashed potatoes

Omit the egg yolks and nutmeg. Mash the potatoes with 75ml (2¾fl oz) potato water or warm milk (dairy-free if required). Season with salt and black pepper and stir in 15g (½oz) butter. **GF V Veg**

fried sliced potatoes

Slice 1kg (2lb 3oz) boiled potatoes into ¾cm- (⅓in-) thick slices. Heat 2 tbsp butter (dairy-free if required) and fry the slices until golden brown on both sides. **GF V Veg**

chips

Cut 1kg (2lb 3oz) potatoes into 1cm- (½in-) thick chips. Wash and dry. Heat a deep-fat fryer to 170°C (325°F) and fry for 4–5 minutes. Drain and leave to cool for 30 minutes. Heat fryer to 180°C (350°F) and fry in batches for 3–4 minutes until golden. Toss with salt. **GF V Veg**

potato croquettes

Omit the butter. Mash and season the potatoes as directed, adding 1 tsp yellow mustard (gluten-free if required). Spread out on a tray to 2.5cm (1in) thick, cover with cling film and chill overnight. Flour your hands and roll into 2.5 x 7cm (1 x 3in) logs. Prepare three bowls: one with 125g (4½oz) plain flour (gluten-free if required), one with 2 beaten eggs and one with 50g (1¾oz) breadcrumbs (gluten-free if required). Roll the logs through the flour, the egg and then the breadcrumbs, then chill in the fridge for 1 hour. Heat a deep-fat fryer to 190°C (375°F) and fry in batches until golden brown. **GF V**

variations

pickled cucumbers

see base recipe page 160

pickled pearl onions

Replace the cucumber with 350g (12½oz) pearl onions. Bring to the boil with the vinegar, sugar, bay leaves and peppercorns; simmer for 10 minutes. Leave to cool for an hour. **GF V Veg**

red, white & green pickles

Use 3 pimento berries instead of the peppercorns. Prepare the cucumbers as directed but do not peel. Put in a bowl with 2 thinly sliced and deseeded red peppers, 1 thinly sliced white or red onion and 1 sliced carrot. Heat the vinegar, sugar and spices as directed. Leave to cool for 10 minutes then pour over the vegetables. Store and use as directed. **GF V Veg**

pickled beetroot

Replace the cucumber with 450g (1lb) beetroot. Roast or steam for 30 minutes, until soft. Peel and slice when cool. Heat the vinegar, sugar and spices as directed, adding 4 cloves. Once cool, pour over the beetroot and leave to marinate overnight. **GF V Veg**

indonesian pickled vegetables (atjar tjampoer)

Omit the bay leaves and peppercorns. Cut 250g (9oz) cauliflower florets into bite-sized pieces. Deseed and thinly slice 1 red pepper, and julienne 2 medium carrots and 150g (5¼oz) green cabbage. Snap 100g (3½oz) fresh green beans into bite-sized pieces. Rinse 100g (3½oz) bean sprouts. Heat the vinegar with the sugar, 2 tsp ground turmeric, and 1 tsp ground ginger, as directed. Add the vegetables and simmer for 1 minute, then transfer to a bowl and leave to cool. Leave to marinate overnight. **GF V Veg**

variations

bechamel sauce

see base recipe page 161

cheese sauce

Stir 150g (5¼oz) grated mature Cheddar or Gouda (dairy-free if required) into the sauce when it is thick and bubbly. Stir until the cheese has melted, but do not bring back up to the boil. **GF V Veg**

parsley sauce

Stir ½ tsp yellow or stoneground mustard (gluten-free if required) and 45g (1½oz) chopped fresh parsley through the finished sauce. **GF V Veg**

mustard sauce

Stir 1 tbsp yellow or stoneground mustard (gluten-free if required), or more if desired, through the finished sauce. GF V Veg

curry sauce

Whisk 1 tbsp curry powder into the finished sauce. **GF V Veg**

sour sauce

Whisk 2 tbsp white wine vinegar or lemon juice into the sauce when it is thick and bubbly, but do not bring back to the boil. Taste and adjust the seasoning. This is great with fish or poached eggs. **GF V Veg**

GF Use gluten-free flour. V Veg Use non-dairy butter and milk.

variations

apple sauce

see base recipe page 162

cinnamon-apple sauce
For extra flavour, add 1 cinnamon stick while cooking the apples. Remove the cinnamon stick before serving. **GF V Veg**

cranberry & apple sauce
Add 100g (3½oz) cranberries, the juice of 1 orange and 1 cinnamon stick to the pan and simmer until the fruit is soft, then stir in the sugar. Remove the cinnamon stick and mash. Optional: add the zest of half an orange. **GF V Veg**

apple & sultana sauce
Wash 75g (2¾oz) sultanas under running water, then soak them in 200ml (7fl oz) warm apple juice or water until they have softened, about 30 minutes. Drain, and discard the liquid. Cook with the apples as directed, adding 1 cinnamon stick when cooking, if required. Remove the cinnamon stick before mashing. **GF V Veg**

apple & apricot sauce
Chop 75g (2¾oz) dried apricots into small pieces and cook with the apples for 20 minutes. Keep an eye on the liquid and top up if necessary. If desired, stir in 1 tsp grated fresh ginger. with the sugar. **GF V Veg**

variations

cheese & onion bread

see base recipe page 165

prosciutto, cheese & onion bread
Cut 120g (4¼oz) prosciutto into strips. Scatter over the dough with the onions, top with the cheese and cook as directed.

cheese & onion bread with honey & chillies
Deseed and chop 1 small red chilli into thin rings. Scatter over the dough with the onions, then drizzle over 1 tsp honey, top with the cheese and cook as directed. **V**

cheese & onion bread with bacon & potatoes
Thinly slice 1 cooked potato and place the slices on top of the dough. Cut 6 rashers of streaky bacon into strips and fry with the onions. Scatter them over the potato slices, top with cheese and cook as directed.

ham, pineapple, cheese & onion bread
Cut 100g (3½oz) cooked ham into small cubes. Drain a 200g (7oz) tin of pineapple chunks. Distribute the ham, pineapple chunks and onions over the dough, top with the cheese and cook as directed.

variations

wholegrain loaf

see base recipe page 166

sunflower seed & wholegrain loaf

Fold 75g (2¾oz) sunflower seeds into the dough after the first rise, setting a small handful aside. Sprinkle over the remaining seeds after the second rise in the tin and cook as directed. **V Veg**

currant & wholegrain loaf

Soak 250g (9oz) currants in warm water, then drain and let air dry overnight. The next day, after rolling the dough into a rectangle, distribute the raisins over the surface before rolling the dough into a loaf. Brush the top lightly with melted butter before cooking as directed, and again when it comes out of the oven. **V Veg**

walnut & wholegrain loaf

Add 75g (2¾oz) chopped walnuts to the dough after the first rise and proceed as directed. **V Veg**

five-grain loaf

Use 650g (1lb 7oz) wholemeal flour and add 25g (¾oz) each of flaxseed, rye flour, barley flour and spelt flour. Proceed as directed. **V Veg**

V Veg Use non-dairy spread.

variations

muesli rolls

see base recipe page 169

apple & muesli rolls
Core and grate 1 red apple. Squeeze as much liquid as you can from it, then add the grated apple and a pinch of cinnamon to the dough in the first mix. Proceed as directed. **V Veg**

apricot & walnut rolls
Omit the muesli. Combine 75g (2¾oz) rolled oats, 35g (1¼oz) chopped dried apricots and 40g (1½oz) chopped walnuts and add to the dough during the second knead instead. Bake as directed. **V Veg**

sultana & muesli rolls
Add 40g (1½oz) sultanas to the muesli and proceed as directed. **V Veg**

spiced ginger muesli rolls
Grate 30g (1oz) stem ginger (from a jar in syrup) and fold it into the dough during the first mixing. Mix 1 tsp cinnamon with ¼ tsp each of ground ginger and nutmeg, and ⅛ tsp each of allspice and cloves, and knead into the dough during the second kneading. Bake as directed. **V Veg**

Veg Use non-dairy spread.

variations

white bread

see base recipe page 170

butter-glazed bread rolls

After the first rise, shape the dough into 15 rolls. Brush with milk before baking for 20 minutes, and brush again with melted butter just as they come out of the oven. **V**

sugar bread

Sprinkle ½ tsp cinnamon and 250g (9oz) pearl sugar or crushed sugar cubes over the dough before rolling. Brush the bread with butter and sprinkle with sugar before and after baking. **V**

raisin bread

Soak 250g (9oz) raisins in warm water, then drain and let air dry overnight. After rolling out the dough, sprinkle the raisins over the surface before rolling into a loaf. Brush the top lightly with melted butter before cooking as directed, and brush again after baking. **V**

dutch cinnamon rolls

After the first rise, shape the dough into 15 rolls. Mix 250g (9oz) brown sugar with 3 tbsp cinnamon in a shallow baking tray. Roll each one through the sugar so that all sides are covered and shape into a log about 21cm (7in) long. Twist the log to create a flat snail shape. Put the rolls on a lined baking sheet, leaving about 2.5cm (1in) between them. Sprinkle a little extra sugar over the rolls, cover, and let rise for about 20 minutes. Preheat the oven to 220°C (425°F), then bake for 10–12 minutes until golden brown. Flip the whole baking sheet upside down onto a clean counter or a sheet of baking parchment and leave to cool. Many people in Zeeland spread a thick layer of butter on the flat side. **V**

celebration dishes

Our celebration of Saint Nicholas, who delivers presents to the Dutch children, on 5 December starts a busy month in the kitchen: between *speculaas* and *kruidnoten* for Saint Nick, we also bake treats for coffee time with friends and for a special Christmas breakfast with the family, and fry treats for New Year. For King's Day on 27 April, a national holiday to celebrate the birthday of our king, the whole country wears orange – even the pastries!

new year wafers

see variations page 216

Kniepertjes are sweet, crispy wafers with which to end the old year and start the new one! On the last day of the year we eat them flat and open, in the same way the past year has now revealed itself fully to us. On 1 January we enjoy the same crispy wafer, but rolled up (see page 216): the new year has yet to reveal all its wonders to us. For this recipe you will need an ice-cream-cone-type waffle iron.

250g (9oz) plain flour
250g (9oz) granulated sugar
1 egg
250ml (8¾fl oz) full-fat milk
1 tsp vanilla extract
115g (4oz) unsalted butter, melted

Combine the flour and sugar together in a bowl, then mix in the egg, milk and vanilla extract. Stir well so that there are no lumps, then stir in the melted butter and the salt. Continue to stir until everything is incorporated, about 3 minutes, then set aside.

Heat a waffle iron, then drop 1 tablespoon batter onto the hot plate and close the lid (or follow the manufacturer's instructions for use). Bake the waffles for 2–3 minutes until golden brown. Use a small fork or a toothpick to remove the waffles from the iron, leave to cool, then store in an airtight container for up to 1 week.

Makes about 40 V

apple beignets

see variations page 217

Deep-fried and battered apple rings are a traditional sight on New Year's Eve, together with *oliebollen* (see page 194) and *sneeuwballen* (see page 228). Use apples that will hold their shape, like Braeburn or Fuji. These are also known as *appelflappen* – though not to be confused with the puff pastry *appelflappen* (see page 252). This recipe makes about 20 beignets, but the quantities can be halved easily for smaller amounts.

4 large apples
100g (3½oz) plain flour
200ml (7fl oz) sparkling water or lager
1 egg
pinch of salt
1 tbsp granulated sugar
¼ tsp ground cinnamon
oil, for deep-frying

Peel and core the apples and slice into 1cm- (½in-) thick rings.

Mix the flour with the sparkling water or lager, the egg and the salt to create a thick batter. Set aside for 10 minutes while the fryer heats up to 190°C (375°F).

Pat the apple slices dry, then use the long handle of a wooden spoon to dip slices into the batter, tapping it lightly so that any excess batter falls off, then let them glide into the hot oil. Fry the apple slices for 2 minutes on each side or until golden brown. Remove from the oil with a slotted spoon and leave to drain on kitchen towel.

Combine the sugar with the cinnamon and sprinkle over the beignets. These are best eaten when warm.

Makes about 20 V

deep-fried doughballs

see variations page 218

Oliebollen are a definite must on New Year's Eve. What better way to ring out the old year than with copious amounts of deep-fried doughballs caked in icing sugar?

275g (9¾oz) raisins and currants (optional)
500ml (17½fl oz) apple juice, rum or water (optional)
500g (1lb 2oz) plain flour
7g (¼oz) dried active yeast
350ml (12fl oz) lukewarm milk or water
pinch of salt
75g (2¾oz) mixed peel (optional)
oil, for deep frying
icing sugar, for sprinkling

If using, soak the raisins and currants in the apple juice, rum or water overnight. The following day, drain and dry on kitchen towel – they should feel dry on the outside, but still plump from soaking.

In a large bowl, mix the flour with the yeast, the milk or water and a pinch of salt until you have a thick batter. Fold in the soaked dried fruits and the mixed peel, if using. Cover the bowl and leave to rise for about an hour, at room temperature, until it has doubled in size. Stir the thick batter once, then cover again while you wait for the deep fat fryer to heat.

Heat the fryer to 180°C (350°F). Without deflating the dough, use a large ice cream scoop or two spoons to take a small ball of dough out of the bowl and put it in the hot oil. Fry for 3 minutes on each side (the *oliebol* will turn itself). Drain on some paper towels, then sprinkle generously with icing sugar. Repeat with the remaining dough. You can cook these in batches of 3 or 4, taking care not to overcrowd the pan.

Makes about 20

V Veg Use water and vegan icing sugar.

king's day millefeuille

see variations page 219

A *tompouce* is a vanilla millefeuille with pink icing – except for on King's Day, when the icing is bright orange, to honour the House of Orange, the Dutch royal family.

1 x puff pastry sheet (approx. 35 x 23cm/14 x 9in)
500ml (17½fl oz) full-fat milk
4 egg yolks
100g (3½oz) granulated sugar
50g (1¾oz) plain flour
2 tsp vanilla extract
100g (3½oz) icing sugar
2 tbsp orange juice
orange food colouring (optional)

Preheat the oven to 220°C (435°F). Line a baking sheet with baking parchment, place the pastry on top and use a fork to prick it at 5cm (2in) intervals so that it doesn't puff up during baking. Top with a second sheet of parchment and baking sheet to help keep the dough flat. Bake for 10 minutes, or until golden. Remove from the oven, remove the top baking sheet and baking parchment, and leave to cool on a rack. To make the filling, bring the milk to a simmer over a low heat. In a bowl, beat the egg yolks with the sugar and the flour to create a paste. Carefully stir 2–3 tablespoons of the warm milk into the paste. Take the milk off the hob and stir in the egg yolk paste until blended, then return to the low heat. Keep stirring until the sauce thickens, 5–6 minutes, then stir in the vanilla extract. Pour it into a bowl, cover with cling film (making sure that it touches the cream) and chill in the fridge overnight. The following day, give the cream a good stir. Cut the pastry into 8 rectangles. Pipe the cream in rows on 4 of the slices, about 2.5cm (1in) high. Top with the remaining 4 slices, flat side up. Mix the icing sugar with the orange juice, 1 tablespoon at a time, and a drop of food colouring, if desired. Spoon over the pastries and spread to the edges. Refrigerate until ready to serve.

Makes 4

GF Use gluten-free pastry and flour. **V**

easter cake

see variations page 220

Easter Sunday is a time when families get together for brunch, lunch or an early dinner. It was also a time when people celebrated the abundance of fresh produce after a cold and dark winter, including fresh eggs and cream. So, how fitting to celebrate with a *paastaart*!

4 eggs
125g (4½oz) granulated sugar
125g (4½oz) plain flour
1 tsp baking powder
350ml (12fl oz) whipping cream
50g (1¾oz) icing sugar
yellow food colouring
250g (9oz) chocolate sprinkles
12 small chocolate Easter eggs, for decoration

Using an electric beater, whisk the eggs with the sugar until foamy, thick and white, 10–15 minutes. The mixture should drop off the whisk in thick ribbons. Sift the flour and baking powder and fold into the whisked eggs. Preheat the oven to 170°C (325°F) and butter and flour the base (not the sides) of a 20cm (8in) springform cake tin. Carefully pour the batter into the tin, trying to retain as much air as possible, and bake for 40 minutes or until golden and springy when touched. Leave to cool on a rack, then remove from the tin.

Whip the cream until stiff peaks form and fold in the icing sugar and one or two drops of yellow food colouring. Slice the cake in half, add a layer of whipped cream to the bottom half, then replace the top. Fill a small piping bag fitted with a rosette nozzle with the remaining whipped cream, and use to cover the sides of the cake. Carefully apply chocolate sprinkles to the sides. Decorate the top of the cake with rosette piping, then finish with the chocolate eggs.

Serves 10

GF Use gluten-free flour and baking powder. **V**

quark cheesecake

see variations page 221

As one of the largest dairy-producing countries, it is only natural to see this bounty reflected in our desserts. A *kwarktaart* is refreshing and a great showcase for seasonal fruit. At Easter, it is often made with fresh strawberries, to lend colour to the table.

75g (2¾oz) unsalted butter
200g (7oz) digestive biscuits, crushed into fine crumbs
7 tbsp granulated sugar
3 gelatine sheets
250ml (8¾fl oz) lukewarm full-fat milk
200g (7oz) strawberries
250ml (8¾fl oz) double cream
1 tsp vanilla extract
650g (1lb 7oz) quark

Line the base of a 23cm (9in) springform cake tin with baking parchment. Melt the butter and mix in the biscuit crumbs and 2 tablespoons of the sugar. Press into the base of the prepared tin. Place in the fridge for at least an hour to harden. Soak the gelatine sheets in water, following the packet instructions. Squeeze out the water and stir into the milk to dissolve. Leave to cool. Slice the strawberries and toss with 1 tablespoon of the sugar. Set aside. Collect the trimmings and cut into small pieces, adding whole strawberries to make about 30g (1oz). Place in a pan with 4 tablespoons of water and 1 tablespoon of the sugar. Bring to a boil, turn down and simmer for 10 minutes. Mash with a fork, and leave to cool. Whip the cream with the remaining sugar and the vanilla extract until it forms stiff peaks. Fold in the quark, then carefully fold in the cooled milk. Pour over the chilled base. Tap the sides carefully to release any air bubbles, then cover with cling film and chill overnight. Carefully slide a warm knife around the edge to loosen, then open the tin and remove the metal ring. Spread the jam over the top, reserving 1 tablespoon, and decorate with the strawberries. Brush the strawberries with the remaining jam and chill until ready to serve.

Serves 10

GF Use gluten-free biscuits. **V** Use vegetarian gelatine.
Veg Use non-dairy butter, milk, cream and quark and vegan gelatine.

almond pastries

see variations page 222

A luxury treat during the winter holidays: puff pastry filled with rich almond paste and decorated with whole almonds. These can be baked as a log (*banketstaaf*) or in the shape of an M, S or an O (*banketletter*) – more out of convenience than for any specific reason, although it is rumoured that the S stands for *Sint* (Nicholas). The almond paste is best made ahead of time and will keep for up to four days in the fridge.

500g (1lb 2oz) blanched almonds
500g (1lb 2oz) granulated sugar
2 tsp lemon zest
3 eggs
1½ tsp almond extract
1 x puff pastry sheet (approx. 35 x 23cm/14 x 9in)
icing sugar, for rolling (optional)

Set aside 16 almonds. Blend the rest of the almonds with the sugar in a food processor to create a paste. Mix in the lemon zest, 2 of the eggs and the almond extract by hand. Divide the mixture in half, shape each half into a ball and wrap in cling film. If the paste is too wet, roll it in a little icing sugar to make it easier to handle. Leave in the fridge overnight.

Using a sharp knife or a pizza cutter, slice the puff pastry sheet in half lengthways. Take the almond paste out of the fridge and roll each ball into a log, slightly shorter than the length of the dough. Place each log on a piece of dough, towards the front of one long edge. Tuck the ends over the log and roll it forwards so that the dough wraps around the almond paste. Brush the edge with a little water and roll it tight. Make sure the ends are tucked in and the almond paste does not show.

Preheat the oven to 200°C (400°F). Line a baking sheet with baking parchment or a silicone mat. Beat the remaining egg in a bowl and set aside. Place both logs seam-down on the

baking sheet. Push 8 of the remaining almonds into the top of each log, spaced equally, and brush the pastry and the nuts with a little of the beaten egg. Put back in the fridge to rest for 30 minutes. Bake for about 20 minutes until golden and puffed up. Slice when cool, making sure every slice has an almond on top.

Makes about 70

GF Use gluten-free pastry. **V**

st nicholas fudge

see variations page 223

These old-fashioned tooth-achingly sugary sweets are traditionally served during the Saint Nicholas festivities. Preparing *borstplaat* is easy and lends itself to plenty of variations. Try one of those on page 223, or give it your own twist!

225g (8oz) granulated sugar
45ml (1 ½fl oz) double cream
¼ tsp vanilla paste

Line a baking sheet or work surface with baking parchment and place 10 heart-shaped or round cookie moulds on top.

Combine the sugar, cream and vanilla paste in a tall, heavy-based pan over a medium-low heat and stir until the sugar has melted, about 1 minute. Continue to stir for another 5–6 minutes. The mixture will start to bubble and spit and will want to rise, making big bubbles on the surface. Remove it from the hob and dip a fork into the mixture – holding the tines downwards,. If the sugary mixture coats them and only a thin thread of sugar drips down, it's ready. If not, return to the heat and stir some more.

Dip the moulds into cold water, shake them off and return them to the baking parchment. Divide the syrup between the moulds, making sure to pour at least 1cm (½in) into each one. Leave to cool for at least 30 minutes, then carefully touch the top to see if the sugar has hardened. If not, give it another 30 minutes – don't be tempted to touch them too soon as the sugar will be extremely hot. When it has, carefully push them out of the moulds.

Makes 10

GF V

spiced almond cake

see variations page 224

Kids anxiously await the arrival of Saint Nicholas for his gifts – and most adults do too, because it marks the beginning of a full month of eating *gevulde speculaas*: a richly spiced cake with almond filling, flavoured with all the warm flavours of the season. Bake it yourself to create that unmistakable, delicious *speculaas* smell wafting from the kitchen.

250g (9oz) plain flour
3 tsp baking powder
2 tbsp *speculaas* spices (see page 214)
150g (5¼oz) dark brown sugar
pinch of salt
150g (5¼oz) unsalted butter, chilled and cubed, plus extra for greasing
3 tbsp full-fat milk
150g (5¼oz) blanched almonds
150g (5¼oz) granulated sugar
1 egg, beaten
1 tsp almond extract

Mix the flour with the baking powder, spices, dark brown sugar and salt in a bowl, and rub in the butter until the mixture feels like wet sand, then knead in the milk for no more than 1 minute until the dough comes together. Divide the dough into two pieces, shape each one into a ball, wrap with cling film and rest in the fridge overnight. Preheat the oven to 170°C (325°F). Set 12 whole almonds aside, and pulse the rest in a food processor with the granulated sugar, three-quarters of the beaten egg and the almond extract to create a loose paste. Line a 23cm (9in) springform cake tin and grease the base and sides. Roll out one dough ball into a 28cm (11in) disc and use to line the base and sides of the tin. Spread the almond paste out over the base. Roll the second dough ball into a 23cm (9in) circle and lay it on top of the almond paste. Press down the edges to join them. Press the 12 almonds around the outside edge, as if they are the numbers on a clock. Stir 1 tablespoon water into the remaining egg and brush the top of the dough. Bake for 40 minutes until cooked through. Leave to cool, then slice into 12 wedges.

Serves 12

GF Use gluten-free flour and baking powder. **V**

spiced nuts

see variations page 225

Kruidnoten, spiced nuts, are also often called *pepernoten*, pepper nuts, although those are of a very different consistency. These *kruidnoten* are hard and crispy. They are usually mixed with chocolate coins, boiled sweets and other seasonal treats to snack on while waiting for Saint Nicholas to show up with gifts.

125g (4½oz) plain flour
1½ tsp baking powder
85g (3oz) dark brown sugar
2 tsp ground cinnamon
1 tsp flaky sea salt
1 tsp ground star anise
½ tsp ground white pepper
½ tsp ground ginger
30g (1oz) unsalted butter, cold
1 egg
milk (optional)

Mix the dry ingredients together in a bowl. Cut the butter into small cubes and add it to the dry ingredients, giving it a quick knead so that it all comes together. Add the egg and knead to create a stiff, but not crumbly, dough; this will take about 10 minutes as the butter will need to soften slowly through the warmth of your hands. If it is too dry, add 1 or 2 tablespoons milk. Cover and leave to rest overnight.

The following day, preheat the oven to 190°C (375°F). Line a baking sheet with baking parchment or a silicone mat. Divide the dough into four equal pieces and roll each piece into a small log, about 1.5cm (⅔in) in diameter. Cut 1cm (½in) discs off the log and roll each one into a ball about the size of a small marble. Place the *kruidnoten* on the prepared baking sheet, leaving a little bit of space between them as they will puff up slightly. Bake for 15 minutes, or until nicely browned. Leave to cool on the baking sheet until cold.

Makes about 70

GF Use gluten-free flour and baking powder. **V**

christmas breakfast bread

see variations page 226

Kerststol, a traditional sweet bread with a rich nut filling, is served at breakfast time at Christmas. The filling is usually whipped out with the tip of a knife and spread over the slice of bread. It is also served at Easter, when it's called *Paasbrood* (Easter bread).

100g (3½oz) sultanas
50g (1¾oz) mixed peel
75ml (2¾fl oz) apple juice (or rum, if preferred)
350g (12½oz) plain flour, plus extra for dusting
120ml (4¼fl oz) lukewarm milk
7g (¼oz) dried active yeast
50g (1¾oz) granulated sugar
1 tsp salt
2 eggs
90g (3¼oz) unsalted butter, melted
1 tsp finely grated lemon zest
icing sugar, for sprinkling

for the filling
250g (9oz) ground almonds
250g (9oz) granulated sugar
1 tsp almond extract
1 tsp finely grated lemon zest
1 small egg

Soak the sultanas and mixed peel in the apple juice or rum overnight. Mix the flour, milk, yeast, sugar and salt in a bowl and let sit for 5 minutes, then mix in the eggs, 75g (2¾oz) of the butter and the lemon zest. Knead well until the dough comes together, about 10 minutes by hand. Cover, and leave to rest at room temperature for 30 minutes, or until almost doubled in size. In the meantime, for the filling, mix the ground almonds with the granulated sugar, almond extract, lemon zest and the egg to create a thick paste. Roll into a log 18cm (7in) long, wrap in cling film and chill in the fridge. If the paste is very wet, it helps to dust the counter with icing sugar and roll it there. Drain the sultanas.

Punch the dough down and knead in the dried fruits. Cover and let rest for 15 minutes. Put the dough on a lightly floured work surface and roll it into an oval, about 20cm (8in) long. Place the almond log in the middle of the dough, lengthways, leaving 1cm (½in) of dough at each end. Fold the dough over the almond filling. Pat it down carefully on all sides, cover,

and leave to rise again for 30 minutes or until almost doubled in size. Preheat the oven to 180°C (350°F). Line a baking sheet with baking parchment or a silicone mat and place the bread on top. Bake for 35–40 minutes until golden brown. From the base, push a thin skewer halfway into the bread. If it comes out clean, the bread is done. Alternatively, you can use a digital thermometer to measure the inside temperature of the bread: it will be done at 88°C (190°F). Brush the bread with remaining melted butter and leave it to cool. Dust with icing sugar.

Makes 1 loaf V

wreath-shaped cookies

see variations page 227

These wreath-shaped cookies, known as *Kerstkransjes*, decorate Christmas trees during the winter holidays. As the days progress, fewer cookies can be found on the tree ... but there will be plenty of crumbs on our faces! To hang them on your tree, thread lengths of red ribbon through the holes.

150g (5¼oz) plain flour, plus extra for dusting
¼ tsp baking powder
75g (2¾oz) granulated sugar
½ tsp vanilla extract
¼ tsp ground cinnamon
1 egg, yolk separated
pinch of salt
100g (3½oz) unsalted butter, chilled
3 tbsp sparkling sugar crystals (or use pearl or demerara sugar)

In a large bowl, mix the flour with the baking powder, granulated sugar, vanilla extract, cinnamon, egg yolk and the pinch of salt. Cut the cold butter into small dice or grate it and knead it into the flour mix by hand until it all comes together, around 30 seconds to 1 minute. Shape the dough into a ball, wrap it in cling film and let it rest in the fridge for 30 minutes. After 30 minutes, preheat the oven to 180°C (350°F). Sprinkle a little flour over your work surface and roll out the dough to about 5mm (¼in) thick. Use a scalloped cookie cutter to cut out 20 cookies. Line a baking sheet with baking parchment and place the cookies on top, then use an apple corer or a large straw to poke out a hole in the middle for the ribbon (optional). These cookies don't spread a lot, but do give them a bit of space.

Slightly beat the egg white until foamy, about 10 beats, and brush the cookies with it. Sprinkle the sparkling sugar on top and bake for 15 minutes, or until golden. Leave to cool on the baking sheet before removing.

Makes 20

GF Use gluten-free flour and baking powder. **V**

profiteroles

see variations page 228

These airy and light profiteroles – or *soesjes* – make great appetisers for a holiday gathering. We serve both sweet and savoury versions – just make sure they are on different platters! The dough and the baked *soesjes* can be made a day in advance.

100g (3½oz) unsalted butter
100g (3½oz) plain flour
pinch of salt
3 large eggs
150ml (5¼fl oz) whipping cream
icing sugar, to taste

Make sure the ingredients are at room temperature. Melt the butter in a pan with 200ml (7fl oz) water, stirring all the time. When the liquid is simmering (not boiling), add the flour and salt and stir with a wooden spoon. Keep stirring quickly until the flour comes together with the liquid and forms a ball, which pulls away from the sides, about 1 minute. Take the pan off the hob and leave to cool for 7–8 minutes. Preheat the oven to 220°C (425°F) and line a baking sheet with baking parchment (grease each corner of the tray so the paper doesn't shift) or a silicone mat.

Add 1 egg to the dough and stir it in until completely absorbed, then repeat with the other eggs, one at a time. The dough should now be more liquid, but still thick. Using two spoons, place dollops the size of large marbles on the baking sheet, leaving approximately 2.5cm (1in) between them. Dip your index finger in water and use it to round out the tops of the dough balls. Bake for 20 minutes, then reduce the oven temperature to 180°C (350°F) and bake for another 10 minutes, or until golden brown.

Take a sharp knife and pierce one of the pastries. If it deflates, it needs to bake a little longer, about 3–4 minutes. If it doesn't collapse, pierce all of them, put the tray back in the oven

and turn it off, cracking the door open a tiny bit. Wait until the pastries are cooled completely before removing. Whip the cream and add icing sugar to taste. Carefully cut the pastries open with scissors or a serrated knife. Pipe or spoon in the whipped cream. Dust with a little more icing sugar just before serving.

Makes 30

V

spiced cookies

see variations page 229

The smell and taste of *speculaas*, spiced cookies, holds the promise of a re-energising morning coffee ritual, a cosy afternoon with friends, or a stolen moment on the couch with a cup of tea and a good book. The warm spices, the crisp texture and the buttery flavour are what make these such a favourite. A windmill-shaped cookie cutter is traditional, but not necessary; any shape will taste fine.

250g (9oz) plain flour, plus extra for dusting
1 tsp baking powder
150g (5¼oz) dark brown sugar
2 tbsp *speculaas* spices*
pinch of salt
175g (6oz) unsalted butter
2 tbsp whole milk

Combine the dry ingredients in a bowl and rub the butter through the flour. Add the milk and knead to create a sturdy dough, about 5 minutes. Wrap in cling film and chill in the fridge overnight so that the spices can blend. The following day, preheat the oven to 180°C (350°F) and line a baking sheet with baking parchment. On a floured work surface, roll the dough out to approximately 3mm (1/10in) thick. Cut out the cookies and place them on the prepared baking sheet. Bake for 15 minutes. The cookies will harden as they cool.

*Make your own spice mix using 8 teaspoons of ground cinnamon, 2 teaspoons of nutmeg, 2 teaspoons of ground cloves, 1 teaspoon of ground ginger, 1 teaspoon of ground coriander, ½ teaspoon of ground cardamom, ¼ teaspoon of ground white pepper. Mix well and keep in an airtight jar for up to 1 month.

Makes 30 cookies

GF Use gluten-free flour. **V**

variations

new year wafers

see base recipe page 191

aniseed wafers
Stir 4 tsp ground aniseed into the batter. Bake one wafer, taste and adjust the aniseed flavour to your liking. **V**

chocolate wafers
Stir 1 tbsp cocoa powder into the batter. Keep a good eye on the time when baking these as it's harder to tell when they are done. **V**

rolled wafers (*rollegies*)
Bake the waffles as directed, but as soon as a waffle comes away from the iron, roll it around the handle of a wooden spoon. The easiest way to do this is to lay the waffle flat on the counter, lay the handle on one end, wrap the end around it and roll it forwards. You have to work quickly as the waffle hardens as it cools. The waffle will be hot, so be careful! You may need to practise this once or twice before getting it right. **V**

rolled wafers filled with whipped cream
Make the rolled wafers (above) as directed. Whisk 125ml (4½fl oz) whipping cream with 2 tbsp caster sugar. Pipe the whipped cream into each end of the rolled wafers just before serving. **V**

variations

apple beignets

see base recipe page 193

banana beignets
Omit the apples. Cut 4 ripe but firm bananas in half lengthways, and then cut each section into three pieces. Use a long metal or wooden skewer to dip them into the batter then lower them into the fryer; do not leave the skewer in the fruit. Fry for 2 minutes on each side, then drain on kitchen towel. Replace the cinnamon sugar with icing sugar. **V**

pineapple beignets
Omit the apples. Drain 2 x 435g (15oz) tins of pineapple rings about an hour before using, and pat them dry. Only use pineapple rings that are firm and without rips or tears. Prepare and cook as directed. Replace the cinnamon sugar with icing sugar. **V**

peach beignets
Omit the apples. Peel and stone 10 firm peaches, and cut them in half. Use a long metal or wooden skewer to dip the peaches into the batter then lower them into the fryer; do not leave the skewer in the fruit. Fry for 2 minutes on each side, then drain on kitchen towel. Replace the cinnamon sugar with icing sugar. **V**

pear beignets
Omit the apples. Cut 5 ripe but firm pears in half lengthways, core and destem, then cut each piece in half again. Use a long metal or wooden skewer to dip the pears into the batter then lower them into the fryer; do not leave the skewer in the fruit. Fry for 2 minutes on each side, then drain on kitchen towel. Sprinkle with the cinnamon sugar. **V**

variations

deep-fried doughballs

see base recipe page 194

apple, cinnamon & raisin doughballs
Omit the mixed peel. Peel, core and grate 2 tart apples (such as Granny Smith). Mix the grated apple with 1 tbsp granulated sugar and 1/4 tsp ground cinnamon and let sit for 10 minutes, then place in a sieve and squeeze as much juice out of it as you can. Fold the apple and 250g (9oz) soaked raisins into the batter. **V Veg**

beer doughballs
Proceed as directed, replacing 150ml (5¼fl oz) milk or water with a dark stout or a fruity beer for extra flavour. **V Veg**

dried fruit doughballs
Proceed as directed, using 325g (11½oz) chopped mixed dried fruits (such as apricot, dates, figs) and chopped walnuts instead of raisins, currants and mixed peel. **V Veg**

cheese & ham doughballs
Use a medium-sized ice cream scoop to shape the doughballs. Replace the dried fruits with 150g (5¼oz) chopped cooked ham, 150g (5¼oz) grated mature cheese and 10g (⅓oz) freshly chopped chives. Omit the icing sugar and serve with a side of mustard.

Veg Use water and vegan icing sugar.

variations

king's day millefeuille

see base recipe page 197

strawberry millefeuille
Omit the orange juice and food colouring. Use 100g (3½oz) strawberries. Pick out 4 strawberries and set aside. Chop and mix the remaining strawberries with 1 tsp granulated sugar. Drain over a colander and catch 1–2 tbsp of the juice. Distribute the chopped strawberries over the cream. Use the juice to make the icing. Make 4 small incisions in each reserved strawberry, fan them out and place one on each slice for decoration. **GF V**

dark chocolate drizzle millefeuille
Omit the food colouring. Use 2 tbsp milk instead of the orange juice, and flavour the icing with ¼ tsp vanilla extract. Melt 40g (1½oz) dark chocolate over a low heat, then remove from the hob and stir in 35g (1¼oz) chopped dark chocolate. Keep stirring until the mixture cools. Dip the tines of a fork or a spatula into the chocolate and drizzle over the icing. **GF V**

almond millefeuille
Omit the vanilla extract. Add 50g (1¾oz) almond paste to the cream with the egg yolks. Use ½ tsp almond extract in the icing. Sprinkle 50g (1¾oz) flaked almonds over the icing. **GF V**

mandarin millefeuille
Drain a 300g (10½oz) tin of mandarins. Set 12 segments aside. Divide the rest over the cream before putting the tops on. Ice and place 3 mandarin segments on each one. **GF V**

GF Use gluten-free pastry.

variations

easter cake

see base recipe page 198

advocaat easter cake
Spread 60ml (2fl oz) advocaat over the bottom layer of the cake. Pipe a little cream over the advocaat, then replace the top layer. Spread another 60ml (2fl oz) advocaat on the top of the cake. Pipe rosettes around the edge and top with the Easter eggs. **Veg**

chocolate easter cake
Cook as directed, adding 2 tbsp cocoa powder to the batter with the flour. Replace the chocolate sprinkles with coloured sprinkles. **Veg**

orange easter cake
Spread 80g (3oz) orange marmalade over the bottom layer of the cake. Pipe a little cream over the marmalade, then replace the top layer. Spread another 80g (3oz) marmalade on the top of the cake. Pipe rosettes around the edge and top with the Easter eggs. **Veg**

lemon easter cake
Spread 80g (3oz) lemon curd over the bottom layer of the cake. Pipe a little cream over the lemon curd, then replace the top layer. Spread another 80g (3oz) lemon curd on the top of the cake. Pipe rosettes around the edge and top with the Easter eggs. **Veg**

GF Use gluten-free flour and baking powder.

variations

quark cheesecake

see base recipe page 201

mandarin cheesecake
Substitute 200g (7oz) Biscoff biscuits for the digestives, and omit the sugar. Drain 2 x 300g (10½oz) tins of mandarin oranges and use instead of the strawberries, using about 30g (1oz) mandarins to make the jam. **GF V Veg**

cherry cheesecake
Substitute 200g (7oz) Bourbon biscuits for the digestives. Discard the cream filling before crushing the biscuits. Pit 350g (12½oz) fresh dark cherries or use 200g (7oz) frozen cherries instead of the strawberries. Use about 30g (1oz) of the cherries to make the jam. **GF V Veg**

peach cheesecake
Substitute 200g (7oz) ginger biscuits for the digestives. Use 250g (9oz) fresh or tinned and drained peaches instead of the strawberries. Omit the jam topping. **GF V Veg**

apricot cheesecake
Substitute 200g (7oz) Hobnob biscuits for the digestives. Use 250g (9oz) fresh or tinned and drained apricots instead of the strawberries. Omit the jam topping. **GF V Veg**

GF Use gluten-free biscuits. V Use vegetarian gelatine. Veg Use non-dairy butter, milk, cream and quark and vegan gelatine.

variations

almond pastries

see base recipe page 202

lemon pastries
Cook as directed, increasing the quantity of lemon zest to 4 tsp and replacing the almond extract with lemon extract or lemon juice. **GF V**

chocolate & hazelnut pastries
Cook as directed, replacing the almonds with blanched hazelnuts. Omit the lemon zest and almond extract and add 2 tbsp cocoa powder. **GF V**

cranberry & apricot pastries
Chop 50g (1¾oz) dried cranberries and 50g (1¾oz) dried apricots into small dice. Mix into the almond paste and cook as directed. **GF V**

walnut, poppy seed & orange pastries
Omit the lemon zest and almond extract. Cook as directed, replacing the almonds with chopped walnuts. Stir 75g (2¾oz) poppy seeds and the zest of 1 orange into the almond paste. **GF V**

GF Use gluten-free pastry.

variations

st nicholas fudge

see base recipe page 204

lemon fudge
Add 2 tsp lemon zest and 1 tsp lemon juice (or 1/4 tsp lemon extract) to the sugar and cream before you start to cook them. **GF V**

chocolate fudge
Stir 1 tsp cocoa powder into the sugar and cream before you start to cook them. **GF V**

raspberry fudge
Stir 2 tsp freeze-dried raspberries into the sugar and cream before you start to cook them, or sprinkle freeze-dried chopped raspberries over the top of the fudge immediately after pouring it into the moulds. **GF V**

coffee fudge
Add 1 tsp instant espresso powder to the sugar and cream before you start to cook them. Add a pinch of cinnamon to the mix. **GF V**

variations

spiced almond cake

see base recipe page 205

coconut & lime cake
Mix 50g (1¾oz) desiccated coconut and the zest of 1 lime into the blended almond paste. Replace the almond extract with coconut extract. **GF V**

pistachio & orange blossom cake
Replace the almonds with 150g (5¼oz) shelled pistachios. Replace the almond extract with ½ tsp orange blossom water. **GF V**

walnut, rum & sultana cake
Soak 50g (1¾oz) sultanas overnight in 3 tbsp rum. Replace the almonds with 150g (5¼oz) chopped walnuts and mix in the drained sultanas after blending in the walnuts. Use rum instead of almond extract. **GF V**

mango & stem ginger cake
Mix 50g (1¾oz) fresh mango cubes and 20g (¾oz) candied stem ginger into the blended almond paste. Omit the almond extract. **GF V**

GF Use gluten-free flour and baking powder.

variations

spiced nuts

see base recipe page 207

chocolate-coated nuts

Chop 150g (5¼oz) good-quality chocolate (milk, dark or white). Melt 100g (3½oz) of the chopped chocolate in a bowl set over a pan of simmering water, then remove from the heat and stir in the remaining 50g (1¾oz), stirring until everything has melted. Leave to cool slightly. Check that the chocolate is ready by spreading a little onto a cold plate and seeing that it hardens. Use a fork to dip the cooked biscuits into the chocolate and set them on baking parchment to dry. **GF V**

coconut-coated nuts

Mix 25g (¾oz) desiccated coconut into the dough and add 1 tbsp coconut milk to bind it all together. Roll each biscuits through another 30g (1oz) coconut and bake as directed. **GF V**

mocha-coated nuts

Add ½ tsp instant espresso powder and ½ tsp cocoa powder to the dough. Add 1 tbsp milk when kneading the dough. Bake as directed. **GF V**

ginger-coated nuts

Pat dry 75g (2¾oz) stem ginger and chop finely. Mix into the dough and bake as directed. **GF V**

GF Use gluten-free flour and baking powder.

variations

christmas breakfast bread

see base recipe page 208

chocolate & hazelnut breakfast bread
Omit the almond extract and ground almonds. Add 250g (9oz) ground blanched hazelnuts and 1 tbsp cocoa powder to the filling, as well as 2 tsp hazelnut liqueur (optional). **V**

mixed spice & walnut breakfast bread
Omit the almond extract and ground almonds. Add 250g (9oz) walnuts and 1 tbsp mixed spice to the filling. **V**

date & pistachio breakfast bread
Replace the mixed peel with 75g (2¾oz) chopped dates or figs (or a mixture of both). Omit the almond extract and ground almonds and make the filling with 250g (9oz) shelled pistachio nuts and 1 tsp orange blossom water. **V**

white chocolate & blueberry breakfast bread
Omit the dried fruits. Replace the lemon zest with orange zest. Chop 75g (2¾oz) white chocolate and fold into the dough with 75g (2¾oz) dried blueberries. **V**

variations

wreath-shaped cookies

see base recipe page 211

almond wreath-shaped cookies
Add 1/4 tsp almond extract to the dough, and sprinkle with 75g (2¾oz) flaked almonds and the sugar, after brushing with the egg white. **V**

lemon & thyme wreath-shaped cookies
Omit the cinnamon and vanilla. Add 2 tsp finely grated lemon zest and a pinch of fresh thyme leaves to the dough. **V**

cranberry & white chocolate wreath-shaped cookies
Chop 30g (1oz) white chocolate and 45g (1½oz) dried cranberries. Add to the dough and mix well. **V**

dark chocolate wreath-shaped cookies
Omit the cinnamon and vanilla. Chop 30g (1oz) dark chocolate into small pieces. Add to the dough with 1 tbsp cocoa powder and mix well. **V**

variations

profiteroles

see base recipe page 212

ham profiteroles
Omit the icing sugar. Chop 75g (2¾oz) ham into small pieces and chop 10g (⅓oz) fresh chives. Fold into the whipped cream and season with a pinch of salt and black pepper.

prawn profiteroles
Omit the icing sugar. Chop 100g (3½oz) cooked and peeled prawns, pat dry and season with a pinch of salt and black pepper or your favourite seafood seasoning. Stir a few drops of lemon juice and a shake of hot sauce into the whipped cream, along with the prawns.

cheese profiteroles
Omit the icing sugar. Fold 100g (3½oz) grated mature Cheddar and a pinch of nutmeg into the whipped cream with salt and black pepper to taste. **V**

chocolate profiteroles
Melt 100g (3½oz) dark chocolate with 100ml (3½fl oz) double cream, stirring well. Keep warm. Drizzle the chocolate sauce over the cream-filled profiteroles just before serving. **V**

snowballs (sneeuwballen)
Mix 75g (2¾oz) sultanas or chopped dried fruit into the dough, right after you've added the eggs. Scoop golf-ball-sized balls of dough onto the baking sheet. Poke in any fruit that may be sticking out and bake for 30 minutes, or until golden, big and puffy. When cool, fill with sweetened whipped cream and dust with icing sugar. **V**

variations

spiced cookies

see base recipe page 214

almond cookies

Chop 50g ($1\frac{3}{4}$oz) flaked almonds and add to the dough. Sprinkle another 50g ($1\frac{3}{4}$oz) flaked almonds over the cookies just before baking. **GF V**

hazelnut cookies

Chop 50g ($1\frac{3}{4}$oz) hazelnuts and add to the dough. Sprinkle another 50g ($1\frac{3}{4}$oz) chopped hazelnuts over the cookies just before baking. **GF V**

chocolate cookies

Add 75g ($2\frac{3}{4}$oz) finely chopped dark chocolate to the dough. **GF V**

almond cookie chunks

Roll the dough out to a rectangle, about 1cm ($\frac{1}{2}$in) thick. Brush the top with a little milk and decorate with whole blanched almonds or sprinkle with 50g ($1\frac{3}{4}$oz) flaked almonds. Bake as directed, leave to cool, then break into chunks. **GF V**

GF Use gluten-free flour.

desserts & baked goods

It is said that the Dutch are some of the tallest people in the world because of their abundant consumption of milk products. With almost 1.5 million dairy cows in the country, it is not surprising that many of our desserts involve milk: whether that is custard, yoghurt, fresh cheese or cold puddings. Besides dairy, we're big coffee drinkers, and with most cups of coffee, we enjoy a biscuit or a small pastry.

bavarois

see variations page 263

Creamy, light and sweet – there are so many delicious aspects to this dairy dessert. It is easy to make and adapts well to each season: think light and refreshing flavours in spring and summer, and warm spices in autumn and winter.

3 gelatine sheets
1 vanilla pod (or 1 tsp vanilla bean paste)
750ml (26fl oz) whipping cream
75g (2¾oz) granulated sugar
2 heaped tsp icing sugar
fresh seasonal fruit, to serve

Soak the gelatine sheets in water, following the packet instructions. With the tip of a sharp knife, split the vanilla pod in half and scrape out the seeds. Add 450ml (16fl oz) of the cream to a pan with the granulated sugar and warm through but do not boil. Add the vanilla seeds and pod. Stir to dissolve the sugar, then squeeze the water out of the gelatine and stir into the mixture until the gelatine has dissolved. Set aside to cool for 20 minutes, but no longer. Whip the rest of the cream to stiff peaks with the icing sugar, then transfer to the fridge until needed.

When the gelatine mixture has cooled, remove and discard the vanilla pod and fold in the whipped cream until well blended. Pour into 8 glasses or a 1.3 litre (2¼ pint) pudding mould. Cover with cling film and refrigerate until ready to serve. To release the bavarois from the mould, dip the bottom quickly in hot water and invert onto a plate. Serve with fresh, seasonal fruits alongside.

Serves 8

GF V Use vegetarian gelatine.
Veg Use non-dairy cream and vegan gelatine and icing sugar.

butter cake

see variations page 264

Butter cake? Well, why not – the Netherlands is dairy country after all. Rich and tasty, the *boterkoek* lends itself beautifully to all kinds of variations, so feel free to come up with your own signature version. And the best part? It's so easy to make!

200g (7oz) unsalted butter, at room temperature
100g (3½oz) granulated sugar
200g (7oz) plain flour
1 egg, beaten
pinch of salt
2 tsp vanilla extract

Preheat the oven to 180°C (350°F). Grease and line a 20cm (8in) round cake tin.

Cream the butter and sugar together in a bowl until light and fluffy, 5 to 6 minutes. Sift the flour and fold it into the mix, with three-quarters of the beaten egg and the pinch of salt. Add the vanilla extract and knead until a dough is formed, about 1 minute.

Press the dough into the bottom of the tin, then use the tines of a fork to run four stripes over the dough from left to right, and four from top to bottom, creating a diamond pattern for decoration. Brush with the rest of the egg and bake for 25 minutes, or until golden brown.

Leave to cool in the pan before slicing into wedges or squares. Leave the cake to cool to room temperature before lifting it out of the pan.

Makes 10 wedges

GF Use gluten-free flour. **V**

coffee-time cake

see variations page 265

It always pays to have a good basic cake recipe at hand. We love a slice of cake with our morning coffee, or to share with our kids when they come home from school.

200g (7oz) plain flour
2 tsp baking powder
200g (7oz) granulated sugar
pinch of salt
100ml (3½fl oz) rapeseed oil
2 eggs, beaten, at room temperature
120ml (4¼fl oz) milk, at room temperature
2 tsp vanilla extract
flavourless cooking spray

Preheat the oven to 170°C (325°F). Use a flavourless cooking spray to lightly grease a 23 x 13cm (9 x 5in) cake tin.

In a bowl, combine the flour with the baking powder, sugar and salt. In a second bowl, mix together the oil, eggs, milk and vanilla. Fold the dry ingredients into the wet ones and give it a few good whisks, about 30 seconds, to make sure there are no lumps.

Pour the batter into the tin. Place on the middle shelf of the oven and bake until golden brown, about 55 minutes. Let the cake cool in the tin for 15 minutes before removing.

Serves 10

GF Use gluten-free flour and baking powder. **V**

spiced cake

see variations page 266

Spekkoek was developed during Dutch colonial times in what is now Indonesia. Making it is a labour of love and patience. Each layer must be baked individually and requires attention, as the thin layers burn easily. It is very rich and often served in thin wedges.

450g (1lb) unsalted butter, at room temperature
200g (7oz) granulated sugar
10 eggs, separated, at room temperature
2 tsp vanilla extract
200g (7oz) plain flour
100g (3½oz) icing sugar
4 tsp ground cinnamon
1½ tsp ground cloves
1½ tsp ground nutmeg
1½ tsp ground cardamom

In a stand mixer, blend 400g (14oz) butter with the granulated sugar until light golden and creamy, 6–7 minutes. Mix in the egg yolks, one at a time, until you have a consistent batter, about 8 minutes. Add the vanilla extract. Sift the flour and carefully fold it into the batter, making sure there are no lumps.

In a separate bowl, whisk the egg whites until stiff, about 10 minutes, then fold in the icing sugar. Fold the egg whites into the batter, then divide it into two separate bowls. Mix the spices with the batter in one of the bowls.

Melt the remaining butter. Lightly brush some of the butter over the inside of a 20cm (8in) springform tin and line the base with baking parchment. Preheat the grill or the oven to 170°C (325°F). Pour a thin layer (about 75ml/2¾fl oz) of the spiced batter into the prepared tin, spreading it with the back of a spoon to make sure it covers the whole base. Place it under the grill or in the oven to bake. This will take very little time, approximately 2 minutes. Brush the baked cake layer lightly with the melted butter, then pour over another thin layer of the non-spiced batter, spreading it out, and return it to the grill or oven. Bake for 1–2 minutes, or

until golden, then brush with the melted butter. Alternate spiced and non-spiced layers, brushing with melted butter in between each layer. When the last layer has been baked, cover the tin with foil and bake for 5 more minutes in the middle of the oven.

Leave to cool in the tin, then remove by running a thin knife along the edge and carefully opening the spring. Wrap the cake in cling film and let it rest for at least 5 hours before serving. Keep it at room temperature or retrieve from the fridge at least 1 hour before serving. The cake will keep for 5 days.

Serves 20

GF Use gluten-free flour. **V**

french toast

see variations page 267

Frugality is at the heart of many a Dutch person, so this recipe for *wentelteefjes* is one that warms our hearts (and our tummies). Don't soak the bread for too long – just enough to allow it to absorb some of the liquid and soften a little bit.

1 egg
250ml (8¾fl oz) full-fat milk
8 slices day-old bread
50g (1¾oz) unsalted butter
2 tbsp granulated sugar
¼ tsp ground cinnamon

Beat the egg and milk together in a shallow bowl, then soak the bread slices briefly in the mixture, about 30 seconds – unless the bread is really stale, in which case leave them for 2 minutes.

Heat half the butter in a large non-stick frying pan and fry 4 slices of bread for 2 minutes on each side until golden brown. Repeat with the remaining butter and bread slices.

Mix the sugar with the cinnamon and sprinkle over the hot toast. Serve warm.

Serves 4

GF Use gluten-free bread. **V**

almond biscuits

see variations page 268

Often called *janhagels*, another name for these delicious cookies was *beddekoek* (bed cookies) as they were traditionally served on the day the mattresses were moved outside during spring cleaning. It was such a heavy task that neighbours and family members would come to help, and for their efforts were treated to coffee and *janhagels*.

200g (7oz) unsalted butter
150g (5¼oz) granulated sugar
2 eggs
250g (9oz) plain flour
pinch of salt
1½ tsp ground cinnamon
1 tsp baking powder
75g (2¾oz) flaked almonds
25g (¾oz) sparkling sugar (or use pearl, decorator's or demerara sugar)

Using a stand mixer or by hand, combine the butter with the sugar until it resembles wet sand. Mix in 1 of the eggs. Combine the flour, salt, cinnamon and baking powder in a separate bowl, then fold into the mix using a paddle attachment or by hand, until everything has combined well to form a dough, about 5 minutes. Wrap the dough in cling film and let it rest in the fridge for an hour.

Preheat the oven to 180°C (350°F). Roll out the dough into a 20 x 30cm (8 x 12in) rectangle on a piece of baking parchment. Beat the second egg and brush it over the dough, then sprinkle the flaked almonds and sparkling sugar on top, making sure you reach the corners. Transfer the parchment to a baking sheet and bake the cookies for 15 minutes, or until golden. Remove from the oven and cut into rectangles. Leave the cookies on the baking sheet until they've cooled and hardened.

Makes 20

V

limburg apricot pie

see variations page 269

The province of Limburg is famous for its pies (*vlaaien*). They originated from leftover pieces of dough that the women would roll out at the communal oven and spread with a little bit of fresh fruit or honey. Limburg pies are still made with a yeast dough and fillings of fresh fruit. This *abrikozenvlaai* uses tinned apricots.

250g (9oz) plain flour
2 tsp dried active yeast
50ml (1¾fl oz) lukewarm milk
2 tbsp granulated sugar
1 egg, plus 1 beaten egg
45g (1½oz) unsalted butter, at room temperature
pinch of salt
1 tbsp dried breadcrumbs
750g (1lb 10oz) tinned apricots, drained
1 tbsp demerara sugar

Mix the flour with the yeast in a bowl and pour in the lukewarm milk. Stir to combine and let sit for 5 minutes, until the yeast starts to foam and appear bubbly. Stir through the sugar, then the whole egg, and finally the butter and the pinch of salt. Knead the dough for 5 minutes or until soft and pliable. Cover the bowl with cling film and leave in a warm spot for 45 minutes until almost doubled in size. Preheat the oven to 200°C (400°F). Grease a 23cm (9in) pie dish or tart tin. Punch down the dough. On a lightly floured surface, roll three-quarters of the dough out to 25cm (10in) and line the bottom and sides of the tin. Pierce the bottom in several places with a fork so that it bakes flat, and sprinkle the breadcrumbs over the base. Place the apricots cut-side down on the breadcrumbs. Roll the remaining dough out to a 23cm (9in) circle and cut it into 2cm (¾in) strips. Drape them lattice-like over the top of the apricots and press them lightly into the dough at the sides. Brush with the beaten egg and sprinkle with the demerara sugar. Bake for 30 minutes, then let the pie cool in the tin for 30 minutes before removing.

Serves 8 V

pancakes

see variations page 270

Pannenkoeken are our thing! They can easily fill up a whole plate, so it's no wonder they're often called cartwheels. Pancakes are never eaten for breakfast, but do make a great lunch or dinner, especially if you choose savoury flavours, but they're also thin enough to roll up after being slathered with jam, or butter and icing sugar or served with fresh fruit.

500g (1lb 2oz) plain flour
1 litre (1¾ pints) full-fat milk
2 eggs
1 tsp salt
50g (1¾oz) unsalted butter

In a bowl, mix the flour with the milk, eggs and salt and whisk well to remove all the lumps. Set aside for 15 minutes.

Heat a little of the butter in a large non-stick frying pan. Pour in enough batter to cover three-quarters of the pan, then swirl it around to cover the whole base. Cook over a medium-low heat for 2 minutes, until the pancake starts to look slightly dry on the top. Flip it over with a spatula, or with a swift flick of the wrist, and cook for 2 minutes on the other side.

Makes 8 large pancakes V

spritz cookies

see variations page 271

The name for these buttery cookies comes from the German word *spritzen*, 'to pipe', because the soft butter dough is piped through a star tip to create round cookies.

200g (7oz) unsalted butter, at room temperature
125g (4½oz) granulated sugar
250g (9oz) plain flour
2 tsp vanilla extract
pinch of salt

Warm a bowl by pouring hot water into it and letting it sit for 5 minutes, then drain and dry.

Add the butter and sugar to the warm bowl and mix together until you have a very soft, creamy consistency, about 5 minutes. Sift the flour and stir in a couple of tablespoons at a time until it has all been incorporated. Then add the vanilla and salt and keep mixing for another 2 minutes. The butter shouldn't melt, just remain soft.

Fit a piping bag with a large star tip. Line a baking sheet with baking parchment and pipe rounds of 5cm (2in) diameter onto the paper, leaving 2.5cm (1in) between the biscuits. Chill the biscuits in the fridge for 30 minutes to 1 hour.

Preheat the oven to 180°C (350°F), and bake the cookies for 15–17 minutes until light brown with golden edges. Leave to cool before removing from the baking sheet.

Makes 25

V Veg Use non-dairy butter.

mini pancakes

see variations page 272

These little puffy pancakes have stolen many a heart! They can be found at fairs and carnivals, served warm on a small cardboard plate, twelve at a time, dusted with icing sugar and with a knob of melting butter on top. *Poffertjes* are made in a special dimpled pan – if you don't have one, you can also make these by using small quantities of batter in a large frying pan; adding the batter to a squeezy bottle makes it easy to portion out.

125g (4½oz) buckwheat flour
125g (4½oz) plain flour
1 tsp dried active yeast
350ml (12fl oz) lukewarm full-fat milk
1 egg
pinch of salt
80g (3oz) unsalted butter
3 tbsp icing sugar

Combine the two flours in a large bowl, then stir in the yeast, milk, egg and salt. Give it a good stir, cover, and leave to rest at room temperature for 30–45 minutes until risen by at least half.

Heat a frying pan or *poffertjespan* and add a little butter to grease the pan.

When the butter has melted, squeeze or pour a little dollop of batter into the dimples (or squeeze about 12 small rounds around the pan) and cook them for a minute or two, until golden brown on the bottom. Flip them over with a fork and cook the top for another minute or two. Repeat until all the batter has been cooked. Divide the pancakes over four plates, or add them to a large platter. Dot the rest of the butter over the pancakes, and dust liberally with the icing sugar.

Serves 4–6 V

dutch apple pie

see variations page 273

Apple pie comes in so many varieties: topless, with a sugary lattice, a double crust, buttery crumble, or a myriad of additions to the filling, such as nuts or dried fruits. It can be deep or shallow, and served with or without cream.

250g (9oz) plain flour
200g (7oz) granulated sugar
150g (5¼oz) unsalted butter
1 egg
½ tsp salt
8 large apples, a mix of two or three varieties such as Braeburn, Golden Delicious, Gala, Pink Lady, Granny Smith or Bramley
1 tbsp lemon juice
1 tbsp mixed spice
3 tbsp dried or panko breadcrumbs
1 egg, beaten
2 tbsp demerara sugar
whipped cream, to serve

Combine the flour and 100g (3½oz) of the sugar in a bowl and rub in the butter. Add 2 tablespoons cold water, the egg and salt and knead together to form a dough, about 4 minutes. Wrap and chill in the fridge for 1 hour. Butter a 23cm (9in) springform cake tin. Peel, core and slice the apples and toss them in a bowl with the lemon juice, mixed spice, 1 tablespoon of the breadcrumbs and the remaining sugar. Set aside. Preheat the oven to 190°C (375°F). Roll out two-thirds of the dough into a 30cm (12in) circle and use to line the base and sides of the pan. Sprinkle the remaining breadcrumbs over the bottom and pour the apple filling into it, making sure the filling is a little higher in the middle. Roll out the rest of the dough and cut it into 1cm (½in) strips. Lay them on top of the apple filling to form a lattice, and press the ends carefully into the dough at the side. Brush the top with beaten egg and sprinkle with the demerara sugar. Bake on the middle shelf of the oven for 50 minutes, or until golden on top. Leave to cool, then remove from the tin. Serve with the whipped cream.

Serves 8 V

arretje's cake

see variations page 274

This no-bake chocolate cake recipe appeared in several cookbooks in the first half of the twentieth century and has been a favourite ever since. It's easy to make and is often the first cake kids will bake with their parents or grandparents, hence the nickname '*oma* cake' (grandma cake). It is very rich and should be served in small slices.

200g (7oz) digestive biscuits
250g (9oz) unsalted butter
65g (2¼oz) dark chocolate
50g (1¾oz) cocoa powder
200g (7oz) granulated sugar
2 tbsp double cream
pinch of salt

Line a 20 x 10cm (8 x 4in) pan with baking parchment or cling film. Break the biscuits into bite-sized pieces.

Melt the butter and chocolate in a pan over a low heat, about 4 minutes. Stir in the cocoa powder, sugar, cream and salt until blended and thick. Stir in the biscuit pieces. Press the mixture into the prepared mould. Wrap with cling film and refrigerate for at least 1 hour.

Makes 12

GF Use gluten-free biscuits.
V Veg Use non-dairy butter and cream and vegan chocolate.

semolina pudding

see variations page 275

Griesmeelpudding or semolina – an old-fashioned dairy dessert – will either bring back great memories or make you shudder! As kids we called it *griezelpudding* (to *griezel* is to shudder) to express our horror, even if we hadn't ever tried it. But now that we've grown up, we're rather partial to it.

800ml (28fl oz) full-fat milk
75g (2¾oz) granulated sugar
1 tsp vanilla extract
100g (3½oz) semolina
fresh fruit and whipped cream, to serve

Combine the milk and sugar in a pan and bring to the boil. Take off the heat and stir in the vanilla extract and the semolina. Return to the hob over a low heat and stir and simmer for 2–3 minutes until the pudding thickens.

Dip a 1.3 litre (2¼ pint) mould or a bowl in cold water and drain, but do not dry as the water will help to prevent the pudding from sticking to the sides. Pour the pudding into the mould and tap the sides to remove any air bubbles. Cover the top with cling film and push it down so that it touches the semolina (this keeps it from forming a skin). Let it cool for 45 minutes, then put it in the fridge for a minimum of 4 hours to set.

Invert the pudding onto a platter and serve with fresh fruit and whipped cream.

Serves 4

V Veg Use non-dairy milk and cream.

fruit turnovers

see variations page 276

Fruitflappen, or fruit turnovers, are traditional triangular pastries made from fresh or frozen fruit and puff pastry. They're quick to make, delicious warm or cold, and the ingredients are easy to keep on hand for unexpected company. The most common ones – *appelflappen* – are made from apples. Enjoy with a scoop of vanilla ice cream.

2 sweet apples (such as Gala)
2 tbsp sultanas
1 tsp granulated sugar
1 tbsp lemon juice
pinch of ground cinnamon
4 x puff pastry squares (13 x 13cm/5 x 5in)
1 tbsp sparkling sugar crystals (or use pearl or demerara sugar)

Peel and core the apples, then chop into small pieces. In a bowl, combine the apples with the sultanas, sugar, lemon juice and cinnamon. Line a baking sheet with baking parchment or a silicone mat.

Brush the edges of the pastry squares with a little water. Add two large scoops of the apple mixture and fold over the dough, shaping it into a triangle. With a fork, push down the edges of the dough, sealing them. Set them on the baking sheet, and when you've finished all four, place the baking sheet in the fridge to wait while the oven heats up. Preheat the oven to 220°C (425°F).

Take the turnovers out of the fridge and brush with a little water, then sprinkle over the sparkling sugar. Bake for 15 minutes on the middle shelf, until puffed up and golden brown.

GF Use gluten-free pastry. **V Veg** Use vegan pastry.

vanilla custard

see variations page 277

One of our most popular dairy desserts is *vla*, a type of pourable custard, which is available in over 50 flavours: from vanilla to seasonal specialities such as stewed pears or *Hopjes*, our famous coffee candy (see page 277). There is something for everyone! For a richer flavour, add 1 egg yolk to the cornflour and sugar mix.

500ml (17½fl oz) plus 2 tbsp full-fat milk
25g (¾oz) cornflour
75g (2¾oz) granulated sugar
1 vanilla pod (or 1 tsp vanilla bean paste)

Mix the 2 tablespoons milk with the cornflour and sugar to form a thick paste, then stir in 100ml (3½fl oz) of the milk, making sure there are no lumps.

Bring the remaining 400ml (14fl oz) milk to a simmer over a low heat. Split the vanilla pod in half and scrape the seeds into the milk, then add the pod. Stir in the cornflour mix and keep stirring while the milk comes to the boil and the mixture thickens to a custard consistency, about 2 minutes.

Remove the vanilla pod and discard. Pour the *vla* into a bowl or individual cups, press a piece of cling film on top (this keeps it from forming a skin) and leave to cool for 30 minutes, then transfer to the fridge to cool further until ready to serve.

Serves 4

GF V Veg Use non-dairy milk.

stewed pears

see variations page 278

Stoofpeertjes (stewed pears) are traditionally made from a local pear variety called Gieser-Wildeman. These pears are only edible when cooked and turn a beautiful ruby red. Since they're hard to find outside of the Netherlands, you could use firm Bosc or Anjou pears. Conference pears will work as well, but reduce the simmering time to under 20 minutes, otherwise they will become soft. Stewed pears are served warm as a side dish, much like apple sauce (see page 162), or cold for dessert with *vla* (see page 253) or yoghurt.

4 large, firm pears such as Bosc or Anjou
1 litre (1¾ pints) cranberry juice
1 cinnamon stick
2 wide strips of lemon zest
50g (1¾oz) granulated sugar
2 tsp cornflour
2 tbsp cold water

Peel the pears but leave the stems on, if possible. Heat the cranberry juice, pears, cinnamon stick, lemon zest and sugar in a pan and simmer for 30 minutes. Carefully remove the pears from the liquid and set aside. Discard the lemon zest but reserve the cinnamon stick.

Mix the cornflour and water to create a thick paste, then bring the poaching liquid back up to a boil. Stir the cornflour mixture into the poaching liquid, stir and boil for 1 minute to thicken it a little, then turn off the heat

Pour the thickened liquid into a bowl, add the pears and cinnamon stick and leave to cool, preferably overnight, or eat warm. Resting the pears overnight in the fridge will ensure that the flavour penetrates the flesh and gives you a pretty red hue all over.

Serves 4

GF V Veg

raisins in brandy

see variations page 270

There have been many preservation recipes over the years, and this is one that has stood the test of time: raisins soaked in brandy. They are delicious as a topping for ice cream or pancakes, mixed in with the apples for an apple pie, or just by themselves in a small glass with a spoon. *Boerenjongens* (which means 'farmer boys') are made with raisins, *boerenmeisjes* ('farm girls') are made with sun-dried apricots.

500g (1lb 2oz) sultanas or raisins
250g (9oz) light brown sugar
1 cinnamon stick
1 litre (1¾ pints) brandy

Wash the sultanas or raisins, then soak them in water for 30 minutes before draining.

Bring 250ml (8¾fl oz) water, the sugar and cinnamon stick to the boil in a pan, stirring until the sugar dissolves, about 4 minutes. Remove from the heat and add the raisins. Let sit for 2 hours.

Pour the raisins and sugar syrup into 4 clean, sterilised glass jars* and pour the brandy on top. Break the cinnamon stick into 4 pieces and put one in each jar. Tighten the lids. Store in the fridge, or in a dark and cool place, for at least 3 weeks before using. Use within 1 week of opening.

* To sterilise the jars, wash them in hot, soapy water and rinse well. Dry the jars in the oven for 15–20 minutes at 140°C (275°F) until hot and completely dry. Boil the lids for 10 minutes, then leave to dry.

Makes 4 jars

GF V Veg

stroopwafels

see variations page 280

These are probably our most popular cookies abroad: two thin waffles with a centre of gooey caramel goodness. They're good cold, or warmed on top of a cup of coffee or tea: the steam will warm the syrupy centre. If you don't have a waffle iron, you can bake them in a non-stick frying pan. Press the dough down with a spatula until flattened, and bake on both sides (but only press on one side) until golden, 2–3 minutes.

250g (9oz) plain flour
125g (4½oz) unsalted butter, melted
pinch of salt
½ tsp ground cinnamon
1 egg
7g (¼oz) dried active yeast
80g (3oz) granulated sugar

for the filling
250g (9oz) golden syrup
100g (3½oz) dark brown sugar
125g (4½oz) unsalted butter

In a bowl, mix together the flour, butter, salt, cinnamon, egg, yeast and sugar and stir until it comes together, 3–4 minutes. Cover and let the dough rise for at least 30 minutes, or until you can see that it has risen. Punch down the dough and roll into small balls, each about the size of a marble. For the filling, heat the golden syrup with the brown sugar and butter in a small pan over a low heat for 5 minutes, mixing well until it has a caramel consistency. Keep warm over a low heat.

Heat a waffle iron. Place a dough ball in the middle and lightly press down on the lid (or follow the manufacturer's instructions for use). Now you must work fast: as soon as the waffle is baked, remove it from the iron and insert the tip of a small knife into the side of the waffle and cut it open. Spread 1 tablespoon the syrup onto the base with a spoon and replace the top. You can leave them rustic like this or use a cutter to make them perfectly round. The cookies will harden as they cool so you have very little time to work with them.

You can also spread the caramel between two waffles instead of splitting them. In that case, press down a little harder on the waffle iron when baking to make them thinner.

Makes about 24 (or 12 if not splitting) V

lemon syrup

see variations page 281

Lemon syrup, or cordial, comes in many different flavours. It's a typical summertime drink, refreshing and sweet. Not many people make their own *limonadesiroop*, but those who do swear by it.

juice of 4 lemons
granulated sugar, measured as directed below
1 tsp citric acid

Pour the lemon juice through a fine sieve to filter out any flesh or pips.

Measure the strained liquid into a pan. For every 100ml (3½fl oz) juice, add 150g (5¼oz) sugar. Bring to the boil and stir until all the sugar has dissolved. Stir in the citric acid.

Leave to cool, then store in clean jars. The syrup will keep for 1 week in the fridge. To serve, stir 2 tablespoons syrup into 240ml (8fl oz) still or sparkling water.

Makes 400ml (14fl oz) **GF V Veg**

mulled wine

see variations page 282

Winter holiday markets, blustery long walks along the North Sea beaches, getting the last of the garden work done before the first frost hits ... a mug of this hot, sweet mulled wine known as *Bisschopswijn* will make all the difference.

1 orange
1 litre (1¾ pints) sweet red wine (Merlot, Zinfandel or a red blend)
4 cloves
4 cinnamon sticks
granulated sugar or honey (optional)

Cut the orange in half and press the cloves into the skin of one half. Cut the other half into even slices.

Simmer the wine with the orange half and slices and the cinnamon sticks for 30 minutes. Adjust the sweetness with sugar or honey before serving. Make sure that each glass gets at least one orange slice and a cinnamon stick to stir with.

Serves 4

GF V Veg Use vegan wine and sugar instead of honey.

wrong coffee

see variations page 283

We love getting together with friends for a cup of coffee or tea. *Koffie verkeerd* (wrong coffee) is what we call our milky coffee.

75ml (2¾fl oz) strong, hot coffee
150ml (5¼fl oz) hot milk
granulated sugar (optional)

Pour the hot coffee into a mug and fill up with hot milk. Add sugar if desired.

Serves 1 **GF V Veg** Use non-dairy milk.

variations

bavarois

see base recipe page 231

biscoff bavarois
Crumble 75g (2¾oz) Biscoff biscuits and fold them into the mixture with the whipped cream. **GF V Veg**

amaretti bavarois
Crumble 75g (2¾oz) amaretti biscuits (vegan if required) and fold them into the mixture with the whipped cream. Add ½ tsp almond extract to the mixture after folding in the biscuits. **GF V Veg**

strawberry bavarois
Chop 150g (5¼oz) fresh strawberries and purée half of them. After folding in the whipped cream, divide the mixture in half. Fold the chopped strawberries into one half of the mixture and pour into the mould. Fold the purée into the other half and pour into the mould. **GF V Veg**

lemon bavarois
Zest and squeeze the juice from 1 lemon. Add 2 tsp the juice to the whipped cream before folding it into the gelatine. Then mix in 2 tsp lemon zest. **GF V Veg**

V Use vegetarian gelatine.
Veg Use non-dairy cream and vegan icing sugar and gelatine.

variations

butter cake

see base recipe page 232

almond & butter cake

Divide the dough in half. Press one half into the pan. Pulse 100g (3½oz) whole blanched almonds with 100g (3½oz) granulated sugar, 1 tsp almond extract and 1 egg, to create a paste. Spread the paste over the bottom of the dough, then press the second half of the dough on top. Decorate with 12 whole almonds instead of the fork decoration and brush with the egg. **GF V**

chocolate cake

Sift 25g (¾oz) cocoa powder into the mix with the flour. Add 75g (2¾oz) dark chocolate chips to the dough. **GF V**

ginger cake

Add ½ tsp ground ginger and 125g (4½oz) chopped crystallised ginger to the dough. **GF V**

lemon cake

Add the zest from 2 lemons and 1 tsp lemon extract to the dough. **GF V**

GF Use gluten-free flour.

variations

coffee-time cake

see base recipe page 235

lemon coffee-time cake

Add 1 tbsp lemon zest and the juice of ½ lemon to the wet ingredients before combining with the dry ingredients. **GF V**

chocolate marble coffee-time cake

Divide the finished batter in half. Add 1 tbsp cocoa powder to one half. Pour the vanilla batter into the pan, then pour the chocolate batter on top and use a spoon to 'pull' the vanilla batter upwards to the top to create a marbled effect. **GF V**

apple-cinnamon coffee-time cake

Peel, core and dice 2 small apples (such as Gala, Pink Lady, Golden Delicious) and toss with ½ tsp ground cinnamon. Add ¼ tsp ground cinnamon to the batter. Sprinkle 1 tsp plain flour over three-quarters of the diced apples and give them a quick stir, then fold them into the batter. Sprinkle the remaining apples on top and bake as directed. **GF V**

speculaas & pear coffee-time cake

Peel, core and thinly slice 1 pear. Mix 1 tsp *speculaas* spices (see page 214) or mixed spice into the batter. Pour half the batter into the tin, add a layer of pear slices, then pour the remaining batter on top and finish with a line of the remaining pear slices. Sprinkle 1 tsp demerara sugar over the top and bake as directed. **GF V**

GF Use gluten-free flour and baking powder.

variations

spiced cake

see base recipe page 236

chocolate spiced cake

Fold 2 tbsp cocoa powder into the batter with the spices. Take extra care to watch the chocolate layers when baking as it will be difficult to tell whether they're getting too dark. **V**

chocolate & orange spiced cake

Fold 2 tbsp cocoa powder into the batter with the spices. Add 2 tbsp finely grated orange zest to the non-spiced batter, and add 1/8 tsp orange extract or flavouring, if desired. **V**

apricot-glazed spiced cake

In a pan, warm 100g (3½oz) smooth apricot jam (blend it if it's in chunks) and brush it over the non-spiced layers after the melted butter. Spread the remaining jam over the top of the cake and dust with 1 tbsp icing sugar. **V**

ginger cake

Add 1 tsp ground ginger to the batter with the spices. Warm 75ml (2¾fl oz) stem ginger syrup with the butter and use to brush the layers. **V**

variations

french toast

see base recipe page 238

french toast with ice cream & dark cherries
Warm 500g (1lb 2oz) fresh, tinned or frozen dark cherries in a pan. Thicken the juice (if necessary) with 1 heaped tsp cornflour mixed with 2 tsp water. Place 1 scoop of vanilla ice cream on top of a slice of French toast and pour over some of the warm cherries. **GF V**

chocolate & hazelnut french toast
Spread each bread slice with ½ tbsp chocolate spread. Top half of the bread slices with 1 tbsp each of finely chopped hazelnuts and place the other slices on top, chocolate side down. Cut, soak and fry as directed. **GF V**

french toast with stewed apples
Peel, core and dice 4 small apples. Simmer the fruit with the sugar, cinnamon, 25g (¾oz) butter and a splash of apple juice or water until soft, about 10 minutes. Stir in 1 tsp lemon juice and serve over a slice of French toast. **GF V**

banana & caramel french toast
Spread each bread slice with 1 tbsp salted caramel spread or sauce. Top half of the bread slices with thinly sliced ripe bananas and place the other slices on top, caramel side down. Press down, then cut into triangles. Cut, soak and fry as directed. **GF V**

GF Use gluten-free bread.

variations

almond biscuits

see base recipe page 239

hazelnut & chocolate biscuits
Replace the almonds with 100g (3½oz) chopped hazelnuts. Melt 40g (1½oz) dark chocolate over a low heat, then remove from the heat and stir in another 30g (1oz). Keep stirring until the chocolate has melted and cooled a little, then drizzle over the baked cookies. **V**

cranberry & apricot biscuits
Chop 25g (1¾ oz) each dried cranberries and dried apricots and mix into the dough. Decorate and bake as directed. **V**

spiced biscuits
Make as directed, replacing the ground cinnamon with mixed spice. **V**

ginger biscuits
Chop 40g (1½oz) crystallised ginger into small pieces and mix into the dough. Decorate and bake as directed. **V**

variations

limburg apricot pie

see base recipe page 241

limburg gooseberry & meringue pie

Replace the apricots with 750g (1lb 10oz) gooseberries. Toss with 2 tbsp granulated sugar, a pinch of cinnamon and 1 tbsp cornflour. Assemble the pie as directed but roll the dough for the top into two thin strands, 70cm (28in) long, and coil them around the edge. Brush with egg and bake as directed. When cool, break up 8 meringue nests and sprinkle over the top. **V**

limburg cherry pie

Replace the apricots with 750g (1lb 10oz) frozen cherries or 1kg (2lb 3oz) fresh cherries (washed and pitted). Toss with 1 tbsp cornflour and 1 tbsp granulated sugar. **V**

butter crumble limburg pie

Use half the quantity of dough and omit the apricots and breadcrumbs. Spread 450g (1lb) cold custard over the dough. Rub 125g (4½oz) plain flour with 125g (4½oz) butter and 100g (3½oz) caster sugar to make a crumble topping and sprinkle over the top before baking. **V**

rice pudding limburg pie

Use half the quantity of dough and omit the apricots and breadcrumbs. Simmer 150g (5¼oz) pudding rice in 1 litre (1¾ pints) full-fat milk with 100g (3½oz) granulated sugar and 1 tsp vanilla extract until the rice has absorbed the milk, stirring. Beat 2 egg yolks with 2 tbsp caster sugar until creamy, then fold into the cold rice. Beat 2 egg whites until stiff and fold in. Pour on top of the dough. Bake for 45 minutes. Whip 250ml (8¾fl oz) whipping cream and pipe rosettes over the top when the pie has cooled then sprinkle with chocolate curls. **V**

variations

pancakes

see base recipe page 242

apple & raisin pancakes
Peel, core and grate 2 apples – 1 tart and 1 sweet (such as Granny Smith, Honey Crisp, Golden Delicious). Squeeze out most of the juice using your hands and stir the grated apple into the batter, together with 50g (1¾oz) raisins. Cook as directed. **V**

apples & bacon pancakes
In a separate pan, fry 150g (5¼oz) chopped bacon until crispy, adding 1 tbsp butter if they don't render enough fat. Peel, core and thinly slice 2 eating apples. Pour the batter in the pan as directed and cook as directed, distributing some of the bacon and apple slices on top. Flip when the bottom of the pancake is browned and cook the other side.

sweet pancakes
After cooking the pancakes, spread a little butter on each one and sprinkle 1 tbsp icing sugar on top, or spread with your favourite jam. **V**

ham & cheese pancakes
Add 75g (2¾oz) chopped cooked ham and 75g (2¾oz) grated mature Cheddar cheese to the batter. Cook as directed.

spritz cookies

see base recipe page 245

dark chocolate dipped cookies

Melt 40g (1½oz) dark chocolate over a low heat, then remove from the heat and stir in another 30g (1oz). Keep stirring until the chocolate has melted and cooled a little, then dip the cookies in halfway. Place on a sheet of baking parchment to set. **V Veg**

ginger & spice cookies

Omit the vanilla and add 2 tsp mixed spice and 2 tbsp finely chopped crystallised ginger to the batter. Cook as directed. **V Veg**

lemon cookies

Add 2 heaped tsp finely grated lemon zest to the batter and cook as directed. **V Veg**

strawberry jam cookies

Place a dollop of strawberry jam in the centre of each cookie just before baking. **V Veg**

Veg Use non-dairy butter.

variations

mini pancakes

see base recipe page 246

mini pancakes with strawberries & whipped cream

Slice and toss 150g (5¼oz) ripe strawberries with 1 tbsp granulated sugar and let sit for 10 minutes. Whip 125ml (4½fl oz) whipping cream with 2 tbsp icing sugar to create stiff peaks. Add a scoop of strawberries and a dollop of whipped cream on top of the warm mini pancakes. **V**

mini pancakes with orange liqueur butter

Mix 100g (3½oz) room temperature butter with 1 tsp grated orange zest and 2 tbsp orange liqueur. Roll into a log and chill. When ready to serve, slice into discs and top each portion of warm mini pancakes with 1–2 slices of orange liqueur butter and a generous dusting of icing sugar. **V**

mini pancakes with chocolate sauce

Melt 150g (5¼oz) dark chocolate in a pan with 10g (⅓oz) butter and 125ml (4½fl oz) double cream to create a sauce. Leave to cool to room temperature and drizzle over the warm mini pancakes. **V**

mini pancakes with rum & raisins

Top each portion of warm mini pancakes with 2 heaped tbsp rum-soaked raisins (see page 276). **V**

variations

dutch apple pie

see base recipe page 248

dutch apple, raisin & currant pie

Soak 100g (3½oz) currants and raisins or sultanas in 250ml (8¾fl oz) rum or apple juice for 30 minutes. Drain then add to the apple filling. **V**

dutch apple & custard pie

Mix 50g (1¾oz) custard powder with 50g (1¾oz) granulated sugar and 75ml (2¾fl oz) milk to form a thick custard. Leave to cool. Pour over the breadcrumbs in the bottom of the pie and add the apple filling on top. **V**

dutch apple & pear pie

Replace half of the apples with pears and cook as directed. **V**

dutch apple, cinnamon & cranberry pie

Add 75g (2¾oz) chopped cranberries to the apple mix and replace the mixed spice with the same quantity of ground cinnamon. **V**

variations

arretje's cake

see base recipe page 249

hazelnut arretje's cake
Roast 125g (4½oz) hazelnuts in a dry pan over a medium-high heat until fragrant and they start to take on a golden colour, about 5 minutes. Leave to cool, then fold into the chocolate mixture with the biscuits. **GF V Veg**

pistachio & candied orange peel arretje's cake
Reduce the biscuits to 100g (3½oz). Add 100g (3½oz) shelled pistachios and 75g (2¾oz) chopped candied orange peel to the chocolate mixture with the biscuits. **GF V Veg**

walnut & fig arretje's cake
Reduce the biscuits to 100g (3½oz). Add ¼ tsp orange blossom water, 125g (4½oz) chopped walnuts and 75g (2¾oz) chopped figs to the chocolate with the biscuits Decorate the top with 10 walnut halves (lay them in the bottom of the mould, flat side up, before pressing in the mixture). **GF V Veg**

spiced white chocolate arretje's cake
Omit the cocoa powder and substitute white chocolate for dark. Add 1 tsp mixed spice, or substitute the digestive biscuits with the same quantity of *speculaas* spices (see page 214) or spiced nuts (see page 207), in which case omit the mixed spice. **GF V Veg**

GF Use gluten-free biscuits. Veg Use non-dairy butter and cream and vegan chocolate and biscuits.

variations

semolina pudding

see base recipe page 251

almond semolina pudding
Add 2 tsp almond extract to the pudding with the vanilla. Sprinkle with 50g (1¾oz) toasted flaked almonds just before serving. **V Veg**

semolina pudding with red berry sauce
Make the pudding as directed. Clean 450g (1lb) redcurrants (or a mixture of red fruits) and simmer with 75ml (2¾fl oz) water and 75g (2¾oz) granulated sugar for 10–15 minutes, or until the berries have softened and released most of their juice. Mash. Mix 2 tsp cornflour with 2 tsp cold water. Bring the fruit to the boil, add half of the cornflour, and stir until thickened. If you want a thicker sauce, use the remaining cornflour. Cool and serve. **V Veg**

raisin & semolina pudding
Add 50g (1¾oz) raisins and ½ tsp ground cinnamon to the pan with the semolina. **V Veg**

stewed apple semolina pudding
Make the pudding as directed. Peel, core and slice 3 eating apples into quarters. Place in a pan with just enough water or apple juice to cover the apples halfway. Add a small piece of cinnamon stick, a star anise and 2 tbsp granulated sugar. Simmer until the apples have softened, about 20 minutes. Remove the cinnamon stick and star anise and serve warm with the pudding. **V Veg**

Veg Use non-dairy milk and cream.

variations

fruit turnovers

see base recipe page 252

rum-soaked raisin & cranberry turnovers
Soak 25g (3/4oz) mix of raisins and cranberries in 50ml (1¾fl oz) apple juice or rum overnight. The following day, drain and combine with the apple filling. **GF V Veg**

cherry turnovers
Omit the raisins, lemon juice and the cinnamon. Use 200g (7oz) dark, sweet cherries instead of the apple. Drain well, and omit the lemon juice. **GF V Veg**

peach turnovers
Use 4 fresh peeled and stoned peaches instead of the apple (or 8 tinned peach halves). Drain well. Leave whole, cut into slices or chop. **GF V Veg**

almond & apple turnovers
To make the filling, core, peel and grate 1 apple. Mix with 100g (3½oz) ground almonds, 1 tbsp granulated sugar and 1 tsp lemon juice into a thick paste. Divide the paste in four equal portions and spread over one half of the dough before folding it over. **GF V Veg**

GF Use gluten-free pastry. Veg Use vegan pastry.

variations

vanilla custard

see base recipe page 253

chocolate custard
Omit the vanilla pod and stir in 30g (1oz) cocoa powder. **GF V Veg**

coffee (hopjes) custard
Omit the vanilla pod. Substitute 100ml (3½fl oz) of the milk with strong cold coffee. Add the sugar to an empty pan over a low-medium heat and let it slowly melt and turn golden. Resist the urge to stir. Mix the coffee with half the milk and dissolve 2 tsp instant coffee in it. Remove the caramelised sugar from the heat and leave to cool a little, then stir the milky coffee into the pan. If the sugar is hot, it may splash, so be careful. Stir, return to the hob, and stir until the caramel has melted. Mix the cornflour with the rest of the milk and stir it into the milk in the pan. Keep stirring while you bring it to the boil and it thickens. **GF V Veg**

lemon custard
Omit the vanilla pod. Mix 2 tbsp lemon juice with the sugar, cornflour and milk. Simmer the rest of the milk and stir in the cornflour mix, as directed. Add the grated zest of 1 lemon. If the acidity of the lemon juice causes the milk to curdle, blitz with a blender. **GF V Veg**

buttermilk (karnemelkvla) custard
Use 350ml (12fl oz) full-fat milk (plus the 2 tbsp) and 150ml (5¼fl oz) buttermilk, and proceed as directed. **GF V Veg**

Veg Use non-dairy milk and buttermilk.

variations

stewed pears

see base recipe page 254

pears stewed in red wine

Replace the cranberry juice with a sweet red wine (red moscato, Shiraz or Lambrusco, vegan if required) and cook as directed. **GF V Veg**

pears stewed in white wine

Replace the cranberry juice with a sweet white wine such as moscato or Liebfraumilch (vegan if required) and add 1 star anise, 1 vanilla pod and 2 cloves. Cook as directed. **GF V Veg**

pears stewed in chai tea

Omit the lemon zest. Replace the cranberry juice with 1 litre (1¾ pints) water and 2 bags of spicy or vanilla chai tea. Simmer for 10 minutes, then remove the tea bags and simmer the pears in the liquid for 30 minutes. **GF V Veg**

stewed apples

Replace the cranberry juice with apple juice (omit the sugar) or sweet white wine such as moscato or Liebfraumilch (vegan if required). Replace the pears with firm apples such as Fuji, cored, peeled and halved. Cook as directed. **GF V Veg**

variations

raisins in brandy

see base recipe page 257

sun-dried apricots in brandy (*boerenmeisjes*)
Use 500g (1lb 2oz) sun-dried apricots instead of the raisins. Use granulated sugar instead of light brown and add a vanilla pod instead of a cinnamon stick. **GF V Veg**

dark cherries in brandy
Replace the raisins with 500g (1lb 2oz) fresh or frozen dark cherries, washed and pitted. Use granulated sugar instead of light brown sugar. **GF V Veg**

mixed fruit in brandy
Replace the raisins with 500g (1lb 2oz) mixed dried fruit (apples, figs, cranberry, apricots). Use granulated sugar instead of light brown and add 2 strips of lemon zest to the sugar syrup. **GF V Veg**

walnuts in brandy
Replace the raisins with 500g (1lb 2oz) walnut halves. Use granulated sugar instead of light brown and add 2 strips of orange zest to the sugar syrup. **GF V Veg**

variations

stroopwafels

see base recipe page 258

chocolate stroopwafels
Add 2 tbsp cocoa powder to the dough and omit the cinnamon. For a double chocolate cookie, replace the syrup in the middle with chocolate-hazelnut paste, and roll the edges of the cookies in 100g (3½oz) finely chopped hazelnuts. **V**

honey stroopwafels
Use honey instead of the golden syrup and make as directed. **V**

salted caramel stroopwafels
Instead of making the filling, use 500g (1lb 2oz) of your favourite salted caramel spread. **V**

banana stroopwafels
Use 2 large, ripe, coarsely mashed bananas instead of the golden syrup. Add 1 tsp lemon juice to prevent them from browning. Combine in a pan with the brown sugar and butter and cook over a low heat until reduced, about 10 minutes. Leave to cool slightly before spreading over the waffles. **V**

variations

lemon syrup

see base recipe page 260

orange syrup

Use oranges instead of lemons. Strain the liquid before stirring in the sugar and citric acid and prepare as directed. **GF V Veg**

raspberry syrup

Simmer 500g (1lb 2 oz) fresh raspberries with 125ml (4½fl oz) water until the berries are soft and can be mashed. Strain the liquid before stirring in the sugar and citric acid and prepare as directed. **GF V Veg**

strawberry syrup

Simmer 500g (1lb 2 oz) fresh strawberries with 125ml (4½fl oz) water until the berries are soft and can be mashed. Sieve the liquid before stirring in the sugar and citric acid and prepare as directed. **GF V Veg**

mixed berry syrup

Simmer 500g (1lb 2 oz) fresh berries (raspberries, blueberries, blackberries, etc). Simmer with 125ml (4½fl oz) water until the berries are soft and can be mashed. Strain the liquid before stirring in the sugar and citric acid and prepare as directed. **GF V Veg**

variations

mulled wine

see base recipe page 261

fruity mulled wine
Add 1 chopped peach, 1 chopped nectarine, 10 halved red grapes and 1 chopped green apple to the original recipe and prepare as directed. **GF V Veg**

white mulled wine
Replace the red wine with a sweet white wine (moscato, Liebfraumilch, Riesling). Add 2 star anise and 2 cardamom pods to the original recipe and prepare as directed. **GF V Veg**

rosé mulled wine
Replace the red wine with a sweet rosé (pink moscato, Zinfandel); omit the cloves. Add 2 star anise, 1 piece of candied ginger and 2 sliced fresh nectarines. Prepare as directed. **GF V Veg**

mulled grape juice
Replace the wine with red grape juice or use a blend of grape and cranberry juice. If serving to children, reduce the cloves from 4 to 2. Add granulated sugar to sweeten. **GF V Veg**

citrus mulled wine
Use red or white wine. Prepare the base recipe, adding strips of zest and the juice from 1 lemon and 1 orange. Just before serving, remove the zests, and stir in 120ml (4¼fl oz) of a citrus liqueur, such as Grand Marnier or limoncello. Taste and adjust the sweetness. **GF V Veg**

Veg Use vegan wine and sugar instead of honey.

variations

wrong coffee

see base recipe page 262

aniseed milk
Omit the coffee. Simmer 250ml (8¾fl oz) milk with 1 tbsp aniseed for 20 minutes over a very low heat. Pour the milk through a sieve to catch the seeds, then add sugar to taste. This is perfect to drink on sleepless nights! **GF V Veg**

chocolate milk
Omit the coffee. Mix 1 tbsp cocoa powder with 1 tbsp granulated sugar in a large mug. Add 2 tbsp milk to make a paste and stir in 225ml (7½fl oz) hot milk until well blended. **GF V Veg**

lemon milk
Omit the coffee. Simmer the zest of 1 lemon in 250ml (8¾fl oz) milk for 20 minutes over a low heat. Add granulated sugar to taste, and remove the zest before drinking. **GF V Veg**

ginger milk
Omit the coffee. Simmer 250ml (8¾fl oz) milk with 1 tbsp ginger syrup and the zest of ½ lemon. Remove the zest before drinking. Add sugar to taste. **GF V Veg**

GF V Veg Use non-dairy milk.

index